CHRIST-FILLED

moments

150 DEVOTIONS *for*
YOUR WALK *of* FAITH

MARK ZIMMERMANN

www.creativecommunications.com

Christ-Filled Moments: 150 Devotions for Your Walk of Faith
was written by Mark Zimmermann for *Creative Communications*
for the Parish, 1564 Fencorp Drive, Fenton, MO 63026. 800-325-9414.

www.creativecommunications.com

ISBN: 978-1-68279-435-7

Design: Jeff McCall
Cover photo: stock.Adobe.com

Printed in the U.S.A.

Practical and Scripture-based, these words and reflections remind us that our God continues to love, forgive and surprise us for ministry to happen to us and through us, as we are assured of his presence in us.

RICH BIMLER, *Ministry consultant; Author of **Joyfully Aging**, **Miracles in the Middle** and **Let There Be Laughter***

Mark has spent a great deal of his adult life writing and editing. All of that experience pays off in these short, winsome, creative devotions that provide practical applications for daily Christian life and growth in faith. If you're looking for an impactful way to supercharge your faith walk, you would do well to spend a minute each day in these "Christ-Filled Moments."

TOM EGGEBRECHT, *Vice President of Ministry Solutions, Lutheran Church Extension Fund; Author of **Fully and Creatively Alive: How to Live a More Joyfully Fulfilling Life***

These devotions anchor us to Christ. They fill our passing moments with the comforting presence of our Eternal Lord. In these reflections upon the Word, we learn what it means to live *in* this world but not *of* this world, as faithful citizens of the kingdom of our Father.

CHAD BIRD, *Scholar in Residence at 1517.org; Author of **The Christ Key: Unlocking the Centrality of Christ in the Old Testament***

Using illustrations from this world, Mark masterfully takes us into the biblical world so we're empowered to faithfully face our world. Everyone looking to enhance their walk with Jesus will be well-served through these timely devotions.

REED LESSING, *Professor at Concordia University, St. Paul, Minnesota; Author of commentaries on Exodus, Isaiah, Jeremiah, Amos, Jonah and Zechariah*

Honest and vulnerable, these devotions tackle real-world problems with God's promised gifts of forgiveness and refreshment.

STEPHEN J. CARTER, *Retired pastor, seminary professor and publisher; Author of My Daily Devotion, Witness to the Light and Heartbeat!*

Christ-Filled Moments is an apt description of these faithful writings by Mark Zimmermann. In these pages, readers will receive respite and refreshment from the toils and challenges of everyday endeavors. The devotions encourage and enliven the reader with a sense of renewal with which to greet the day.

DAVID MEGGERS, *Associate Pastor, Concordia Lutheran Church, Kirkwood, MO*

We live in disorienting times. It seems like change and challenge are coming at us from every direction. The brief, user-friendly devotions in *Christ-Filled Moments* point readers toward Jesus, who longs to reorient us to what matters most and awaken us to his work in this world.

MICHELLE VAN LOON, *Author of Translating Your Past: Finding Meaning in Family Ancestry, Genetic Clues, and Generational Trauma*

Mark's eyes of faith remain focused on finding Christ-filled, teachable moments in everyday life. He gives significance to what we often see as insignificant. I'm certain the Holy Spirit will use these faith-strengthening devotions to teach us to see and seize Christ-filled moments in our lives.

TIM WESEMANN, *Author of Swashbuckling Faith and Jack Bauer's Having a Bad Day*

Thought-provoking and insightful, these devotions are truly relevant and real. Using topics we can all relate to, Mark has a gift of meaningfully weaving Christ on the cross into everyday living. Each one makes me want to read the next.

JANE WILKE, *Director of Church Relations, Concordia University, St. Paul, MN*

INTRODUCTION

*May the God of endurance and encouragement grant you
to live in such harmony with one another, in accord with
Christ Jesus, that together you may with one voice glorify
the God and Father of our Lord Jesus Christ.* ROMANS 15:5-6

What an encouragement it is to know that Christ is present with us. It is his presence with us that infuses circumstances and situations with meaning and purpose. Many times we can't see him very clearly, and at other times we have the very strong sense that he is close beside us. Those powerful times are what we call Christ-filled moments. This collection of 150 devotions is designed to help you see Christ filling many of the moments of your life in the simplest of things. When we sharpen our focus on Christ's presence, we become even more aware of the influence of Christ in our everyday living. During his time on earth, Jesus touched the lives of thousands with his words of promise, acts of healing, miraculous signs and works of service. And he is still touching our lives in similar ways today, bringing harmony, comfort, hope and peace.

These reflections can be read any time in any order in any way you wish. Simply open this book anywhere along your walk of faith, and you will find Christ on every page. Draw near to him as he draws near to you.

Mark Zimmermann, AUTHOR

New Year Visions

On the cusp of a new year, we like to envision a fresh start, a change for the better, a bright future. We often put all our hopes and dreams on a new year. There is nothing wrong with that, as long as we recognize that life does not always go the way we planned. We may be disappointed on any one of the 365 days to come.

As Christians, we put our hopes and dreams on Christ and not on a particular set of days. Every morning is a new start because of his forgiveness. Every day is a new opportunity to serve him. Every 24-hour period is a gift from our Savior, who died that we might live for him. There will be troubles and detours and unexpected bumps in the road, but our confidence in our risen Lord assures us that we will grow and learn and become stronger because of his presence with us.

"We are to grow up in every way into him who is the head, into Christ" (Ephesians 4:15). No matter what your age, make growing up into Christ your goal for the year. He will make it happen!

FOR REFLECTION

How can you grow in your relationship with Christ today?

CHRIST-FILLED MOMENTS

The Light from Afar

The wise men followed the star from afar. They did not stop until they came to the palace in Jerusalem where they thought Jesus was born a king. But the chief priests and scribes pointed them in the direction of Bethlehem, where, according to the Scriptures, the wise men found the Christ Child. (See Matthew 2.)

The wise men followed the Word after they followed the star. It was the Word that put them back on course. It was the Word that led them to Jesus, the Star of their lives. And it is the Word that leads us, too, to Jesus, who is the Star of our lives too. As the psalmist says, "Your word is a lamp to my feet and a light to my path" (Psalm 119:105).

The star the wise men saw is no longer present in the sky, but the light of the Word remains today. All we need to do is open the pages of Scripture to see it. The Word enlightens our lives with hope, faith and love. It is the Word that brings us close to the Light of the World, Jesus, our Savior. He shines on us with forgiveness through his death and resurrection and guides us on to everlasting life with him.

FOR REFLECTION

In what way can you be led by the Word today?

Water and the Word

My parents recently reminded me that I was baptized using water my grandparents brought from the Jordan River on their trip to the Holy Land. I was touched and moved by this forgotten news, but it got me to thinking that, when it comes to baptism, the source of the water does not really matter.

What matters is the connection of that water to the Word. This Word is spoken over the baptized person as water is poured: "I baptize you in the name of the Father and of the Son and of the Holy Spirit." The Word of God reminds us: "This water symbolizes baptism that now saves you also—not the removal of dirt from the body but the pledge of a clear conscience toward God. It saves you by the resurrection of Jesus Christ" (1 Peter 3:21, NIV®).

Through baptism, we are made brothers and sisters of Jesus, the Word made flesh. Through the work of the Holy Spirit, it is in this Word that we find our hope, with the sprinkling of water, whatever its source.

FOR REFLECTION

What reminds you of your baptism?

CHRIST-FILLED MOMENTS

White as Snow

*Though your sins are like scarlet, they shall
be as white as snow.* ISAIAH 1:18

Many of us have experienced monster snowstorms, often
multiple snowstorms in a row. The aftermath of such storms
can be difficult and frustrating, but people also report on the
beautiful sight of the snow falling, as their yards are slowly
covered over. As I thoroughly enjoyed just sitting and watching the snow softly falling out my living room window one
February, I wondered: Why this response? I think it has something to do with the feeling of everything becoming fresh and
new. There is a sense that all the world is clean and bright.

Isaiah must have known the comfort of freshly fallen snow
when he compared it to the forgiveness of sins. When we take our
sins to God, they are completely covered over, snowflake upon
snowflake. It is said that no two snowflakes are alike. Through the
suffering and death of Jesus Christ, God's forgiveness makes sure
that no sin is left uncovered by his grace and mercy.

The next time you find yourself looking out at a snowfall, think
of the blessings of forgiveness that fall down on us every day,
forgiveness that renews our lives with the beauty of God's gift.

FOR REFLECTION

When have you last experienced the joy of a snowfall?

Water Into Wine

In his first miracle, Jesus turned water into wine at the wedding of Cana, and the wedding guests continued celebrating. This miracle foreshadowed the Lord's Supper and revealed the transformation of his people.

Jesus' mother Mary told her son, "They have no wine" (John 2:3). She knew that Jesus could solve the problem. She told the servants, "Do whatever he tells you" (John 2:5). Jesus was the one to whom they should listen. Without wine, the celebration would end, but the feast continued when Christ provided wine. The marriage feast is a symbol of the feast of heaven, where the Groom, Christ, weds his Bride, the Church, in a celebration that will last forever.

The miraculous wine from water was "the best," but a better wine was poured at the Lord's table the night before his death. That wine was the blood of Christ, shed for the forgiveness of our sins. The wine at the Lord's Supper brings a deeper celebration of everlasting joy through the removal of sins. The wine poured at Cana flowed through Christ's ministry to the wine of the Lord's Supper, wine that flows to us as we partake of the bread and wine of Holy Communion. This very best of wine—the blood of our Savior—enters us in a rich and abundant way.

FOR REFLECTION

How have you been enriched by the blood of Christ?

Candy Hearts

As a kid, on Valentine's Day, I enjoyed getting candy hearts and reading the messages: "I love you," "Be mine," "True love," "My pal" and "Friends forever." We eat the candy and then don't think much about the words, but these candy hearts have a very biblical connection:

> And you show that you are a letter from Christ
> delivered by us, written not with ink but with the
> Spirit of the living God, not on tablets of stone but
> on tablets of human hearts. 2 CORINTHIANS 3:3

God has imprinted his love and care on our hearts. He truly means it when he says, "I love you," "Be mine," "True love," "My pal" and "Friends forever." These divine messages on our hearts define who we are and whose we are. These words should motivate us in our love for one another: "We love because he first loved us" (1 John 4:19). His love for us helps us to say, "I love you," "Be mine," "True love," "My pal" and "Friends forever" in the Lord's name to one another. With sincere hearts, we care for one another in the same way that God cares for us. Let every heart be a message board of love.

FOR REFLECTION

What messages of love would you like to share today?

Are You Facing Out?

For Jews demand signs and Greeks seek wisdom,
but we preach Christ crucified ... 1 CORINTHIANS 1:22-23

When my father graduated from the seminary, my mother gave him a ring with a cross at the center. But in his first weeks as a new pastor in Odell, Nebraska, a farmer observed, "You're wearing that ring all wrong. You have it so the cross is facing you. The cross should be facing out to the people you meet." My dad has been wearing that ring facing out ever since.

It's tempting to treat Christ's cross as something that is just for us. We can look at it as a personal memento or a secret comfort. Is that God's desire? The message of forgiveness and heaven is meant to be something that we share prodigally in our daily lives. The cross of Christ should be "facing out" in the way we love, forgive and care for others as Christ loves, forgives and cares for us.

FOR REFLECTION

In what ways can you reach out to someone with the cross?

CHRIST-FILLED MOMENTS

Recharging

Everyone is obsessed with keeping their smartphones charged. Our greatest fear is being somewhere without a fully charged phone. While I know from experience that lost feeling of being in the middle of nowhere with a dead phone, I wonder what our obsession with charging our phones says about our priorities.

We are not nearly as diligent about recharging our faith on a daily basis. If we have the time to search for an outlet to recharge our phones, we certainly have the time to search through Scripture throughout the day to charge ourselves spiritually.

Instead of panicking when we receive notification that our phone power is at 20% and then at 10%, we should be worried if we have made it through 10% or 20% of the day without praying. Our spirits can be refreshed with a few moments of one-on-one conversation with our Savior. If we can drop everything to find our charger or dig around the car for that USB cord, we can certainly have the same sort of urgent approach when we are in desperate need of a reconnection with the divine.

Every day we can recharge our faith through prayer, Bible study, meditation and reflection. It should be an obsession!

FOR REFLECTION

What part of your life needs the most recharging?

The Day of Small Things

For whoever has despised the day of small things shall rejoice ... **ZECHARIAH 4:10**

Sometimes I feel like I am immersed in "small things" every day, the mundane tasks that must be done—doing laundry, paying bills, cooking meals, mowing the lawn, putting gas in the car and running errands. Small things can wear me down. I find solace in the fact that Zechariah acknowledges those who have "despised the day of small things." I am not alone! Zechariah assures us that we despisers of small things will rejoice because the eyes of the Lord will "range through the whole earth" (Zechariah 4:10). Our Lord is taking care of the big picture, making sure that his grand plan for all things is coming together.

We are on a forward-moving trajectory that is taking us ever closer to the hallways of heaven, where the purpose of all the small things in life will be revealed at the throne of our crucified and risen Lord Jesus Christ. For us he became small so that we might live large in his presence forever.

So don't be frustrated by the small things. Those small things are bringing us ever closer to the Last Day, when we will live life to the fullest for all eternity.

FOR REFLECTION

What "small thing" can you rejoice in today?

Strength You Have

The LORD turned to [Gideon] and said, "Go in the strength you have and save Israel out of Midian's hand. Am I not sending you?" **JUDGES 6:14 (NIV®)**

When I was feeling over-busy and bedraggled, the words "go in the strength *you have*" really registered with me, giving me hope and confidence that I could accomplish the multiple tasks that lay before me. I may not feel the strongest I have ever felt, but God has given me the strength I *do have* to do great things.

This verse is also a message from God telling me that he is sending me. He knows the challenges I face and he will not abandon me to go it alone. He has faith in me to carry out the mission he has for me. He knows my capabilities better than I do and, if I run into any trouble, he will be there to get me through it.

In the mornings when I haven't felt much like getting up when the alarm goes off, I simply say to myself, "Go in the strength you have." That gets me moving to start the day.

FOR REFLECTION

What do you need strength for?

Provenance

In the art world, the term *provenance* refers to the history of ownership of a work of art. Museum curators go to great lengths to determine who owned a particular piece and when. The more known about the history of a painting and its owners, the greater the value of the masterpiece.

As God's masterpieces, we do not have to track down our provenance. Since baptism we have had one owner: God. We belong to him, and we are more precious to him than the *Mona Lisa*. As the Bible says,

> *Fear not, for I have redeemed you; I have called you by name, you are mine.*   ISAIAH 43:1

So what do we do with this information?

> *For you were bought with a price. So glorify God in your body.*   1 CORINTHIANS 6:20

All we say and do with these works of art we call our bodies must be to God's glory, to honor the One who crafted and designed us and purchased us at great cost. Each word and action is like a divine brushstroke guided by the hand of the Master. We may not be museum quality, but because of Christ and his cross, we have a place designated for us in the halls of heaven.

FOR REFLECTION

Why is it good for you to know that you have a place with God?

Letters

You yourselves are our letter of recommendation, written on our hearts, to be known and read by all. And you show that you are a letter from Christ delivered by us, written not with ink but with the Spirit of the living God, not on tablets of stone but on tablets of human hearts. **2 CORINTHIANS 3:2-3**

We don't write letters too much anymore, but in the early Church, handwritten letters were the only way to receive information from a great distance. The epistles were originally simply letters from one friend to another group of friends, talking about the life of faith in Christ. Today those letters are studied and valued for their importance in guiding our lives as Christians.

Letters were so important to the early Christians that Paul refers to those who receive his actual letter as letters themselves. We, too, as recipients of Paul's letters, are letters. We are not letters written with ink that fades, but we are written with the Spirit of the living God. We have vibrancy and force that will last forever. We are not written on cold and unfeeling stone. We are letters written on beating human hearts that supply lifeblood to the world.

FOR REFLECTION

To whom would you like to write a letter?

Dishes

When I bought my house, I was not concerned that it did not have a dishwasher. But I did not realize how often I would be washing plates and cups and silverware again and again. The Bible has a lot to say about dishwashing. The Pharisees in Jesus' day were apparently very good at doing dishes: "There are many other traditions that they observe, such as the washing of cups and pots and copper vessels and dining couches" (Mark 7:4). Jesus used the practice to teach us about spiritual disciplines: "Woe to you, scribes and Pharisees, hypocrites! For you clean the outside of the cup and the plate, but inside they are full of greed and self-indulgence. You blind Pharisee! First clean the inside of the cup and the plate, that the outside also may be clean" (Matthew 23:25-26).

I may think my oatmeal bowls are clean, but inside I find flecks of crusted oats. We can put on a good front of a Christian life, but caked-on sins make us unclean inside. If unclean thoughts creep into my mind, I make a point through the power of Christ to rid myself of those "crusty" thoughts and engage my mind in God-pleasing thoughts. Those "clean" thoughts show on the outside in sincere faith practices and acts of Christlike kindness toward others.

FOR REFLECTION

What do you want to clean out of your life?

Struck Down but Not Destroyed

I love the language of 2 Corinthians 4:8-9:

We are hard pressed on every side, but not crushed. We are pressed from every angle with the demands of work, family, home and church, but we are not crushed. Nothing can be a crushing blow when we have Christ within us.

Perplexed, but not in despair. We may be confused, frustrated or angry about our lives, but we should never let that angst turn into despair, tempting us to give up on God, on ourselves or on others. We cannot throw in the towel when God is fighting for us.

Persecuted, but not abandoned. For the early Christians in Corinth, persecution was a real threat. Suffering is a given for Christians in this world. Sin and the devil will make sure of that! But we will never be left alone to fend for ourselves. The Triune God loves us and comforts us in every struggle. Our God will never go away.

Struck down but not destroyed. We may be struck down by illness, a harsh word or rejection. We will be knocked down, but we will never be obliterated. Isaiah tells us that God will not snuff out even a dimly burning wick. Christ destroyed the powers of death, sin and the devil through his life, death and resurrection. He will never destroy us.

FOR REFLECTION

What words in these verses impact you the most?

Visual Storytelling

In the Middle Ages, stained-glass windows told the story of salvation to the many illiterate people in the pews. Today there is a resurgence of visual storytelling, most notably through social media sites like Instagram. The goal of Instagram is to share photos of your life with others. As a Christian, then, your Instagram posts can serve as stained-glass windows displaying your life in Christ to the world.

What images are you sharing? What can people learn about you from the pictures you put up on your Instagram or Facebook page? Take a quick look at your image-posting history. Can people see that you are a Christian from these images? If so, then great! If not, what can you include in future image postings that reveal your commitment to Christ and the central role he plays in your life?

So much of social media imagery is about me, myself and I. But as Christians we say it is all about him as we point to Jesus Christ in our social media stained-glass windows.

FOR REFLECTION

What specific visuals point to Jesus in your life?

Encouragement

Joseph, a Levite from Cyprus, whom the apostles called
Barnabas (which means "son of encouragement"),
sold a field he owned and brought the money and
put it at the apostles' feet. ACTS 4:36-37 (NIV®)

Throughout the Book of Acts, we read about a disciple of Christ named Barnabas, whose name means "son of encouragement." His name indicates the impact he had on the early Church and to those to whom he witnessed on his many missionary trips with the apostle Paul.

How can you be a Barnabas, a son or daughter of encouragement, in your life today? You can be on the lookout, as Barnabas was, for the gifts in others. Then encourage people to use those gifts to God's glory. Don't be afraid to join them in using your gifts, standing beside them to support them along the way. You can be encouraging by being open and available when people want to talk, as Barnabas was. Be there to listen. Be there to care. Be there to take an interest in the lives of people. Keep urging them on in their work for the Lord and in living in God's grace.

To whom can you be a Barnabas today?

FOR REFLECTION

Who has encouraged you in your faith?

Adiaphora

The word *adiaphora* means "matters not regarded as essential to faith, but nevertheless permissible or allowed in the church." Topics such as the floor covering in the sanctuary or the color of the paint on the walls of the fellowship hall, for example, are not essential to faith, but often take up a large part of our time. Adiaphora.

St. Paul was asked about adiaphora by the Corinthian Christians. Should they eat food sacrificed to idols? He said in response: Food does not bring us near to God; we are no worse if we do not eat, and no better if we do. Be careful, however, that the exercise of your freedom does not become a stumbling block to the weak. (See 1 Corinthians 8:8-9.)

We need to spend less time worrying about things that are essentially adiaphora and more time on matters that are essential to faith: Baptism, evangelism, Holy Communion, preaching the Word, Bible study and prayer. Even if something we do or say is not necessarily against our beliefs, we need to be aware of the way in which we go about these things. We are models of Christ even in things that don't really matter.

FOR REFLECTION

What matters of faith can you focus on more fully?

Cairns

While hiking in Rocky Mountain National Park, I noticed stones stacked up into little towers called cairns that served as landmarks and memorials. Cairns are similar to the rock formations used in the Bible by Abraham, Moses and Jacob as altars.

Abraham built an altar to acknowledge that God is God, saying through this cairn that he would obey God's will. God sent an angel to stop Abraham from sacrificing his son. Centuries later, God would sacrifice his own Son, Jesus, on the altar, the cairn, if you will, of a cross on a rock hill called Golgotha.

Moses erected an altar to God after the Israelites defeated the army of Amalek. We have moments in our lives after a trial or tragedy, when we, like Moses, need to step back and honor in some special way the God who got us through.

The morning after Jacob dreamed of angels ascending and descending a stairway to heaven, he used a stone to make a cairn to announce that this was a dwelling place of God. We need to remember, too, that though we are sinners, God still loves us and has a plan of salvation for us, to take us to heaven to be with him forever.

Honor the Lord, who is the Rock, on your journey through life.

FOR REFLECTION

At what times in your life did you stop to worship God?

Judge Not

"Judge not, and you will not be judged," Jesus clearly states (Luke 6:37). But that is easier said than done when we are living in an increasingly judgmental society. It is easy to join the chorus of voices judging others.

As the saying goes, every time you point one finger at someone, there are three fingers pointing back at you. We are all sinners, and we all fail. As Christians, we need to replace the judgments that may be welling up inside of us with forgiveness and love. That is how we would like to be treated if the roles were reversed.

Jesus continues, "Condemn not, and you will not be condemned; forgive, and you will be forgiven" (Luke 6:37). It is not our place to condemn. That is up to God. But it is our role to forgive. We are all in need of Christ's mercy for our failings, big or small. Our role as Christians is not to point to people in judgment but to point people to the cross. Only there can grace be found.

FOR REFLECTION

What judgmental thought is nagging at you now?

The Image of God

"So God created mankind in his own image, in the image of God he created them" (Genesis 1:27, NIV®). Many wonder exactly what "the image of God" means. Some think it refers to our ability to reason. Another view suggests that God is reflected in our physical characteristics. Still others think the image of God refers to our relational nature and the relationships we have with God and creation.

I tend to favor the last description. God gave human beings a special place in the world. He desires a close, personal bond with us. His love for us is on a much deeper level than his care for plants and animals.

God gave us a special place in his heart: "I have loved you with an everlasting love" (Jeremiah 31:3). Out of his great love, he sent Jesus to save us. Peter reminds us that, through Christ, "You are a chosen people, a royal priesthood, a holy nation, God's special possession, that you may declare the praises of him who called you out of darkness into his wonderful light" (1 Peter 2:9, NIV®). That is our role as people created in God's image: We are to declare his praises and imitate him. Let the image of God shine through you.

FOR REFLECTION

How do people see the image of God in you personally?

Sinking Down

On a recent trip with friends, I slept on an air mattress. Unfortunately, there was a leak in the mattress. By morning, I had sunk down into the middle with the two sides of the mattress enfolding me like a taco, which brought peals of laughter from my friends.

I remembered the hymn "What Wondrous Love Is This": "When I was sinking down, sinking down, sinking down ... Christ laid aside his crown for my soul."

It was hard for me to get out of the "sunken down" mattress. It is impossible to free myself when I am sunken down in sin. Only Christ can lift me out. I also noticed that "down low" there was still a bit of air left in the mattress; I was not sleeping directly on the floor. When I think I have reached rock bottom in my life, I must always remember that the breath of the Holy Spirit still lifts me and sustains me, keeping me from the pit of despair. The sides of that sunken mattress acted like a warm hug, like a loving Father, who says to me, "Don't worry. I've got you. You will not be crushed by sin."

The next night I slept on a fully-pumped air mattress with no leaks, and all was right with the world.

FOR REFLECTION

What lifts you up when you are sinking down?

Redeem

The word *redeem* had legal meaning in Old Testament Hebrew. The term meant to buy back a person, property or right to which one had a previous claim. Someone who had to sell himself into slavery because of poverty, for instance, could have his freedom bought back by someone called a redeemer, usually his next of kin.

Boaz redeemed the widow Ruth when he bought back the land that belonged to her mother-in-law, the widow Naomi. Boaz said, "You are witnesses this day that I have bought from the hand of Naomi all that belonged to Elimelech and all that belonged to Chilion and to Mahlon. Also Ruth the Moabite, the widow of Mahlon, I have bought to be my wife, to perpetuate the name of the dead in his inheritance, that the name of the dead may not be cut off from among his brothers and from the gate of his native place" (Ruth 4:9-10).

This foreshadows the way Christ redeemed the Church and bought it back as his Bride. He saw our lost state and made sure we had a family, a home and a relationship with him. And the payment for this redemption? The body and blood of Jesus. He gave completely of himself to give us an inheritance with him forever. What a glorious transaction!

FOR REFLECTION

How does it feel to be bought back by Christ?

Broken and Restored

There is a centuries-old Japanese method of repairing broken pottery called *kintsugi* (which means "golden joinery") or *kintsukuroi* (which means "golden repair"). Pieces of broken pottery are joined with a special lacquer dusted with gold, silver or platinum. Beautiful trails of gold sparkle where cracks once existed, creating an interesting effect. The method can take a long time to complete, but the results are stunning.

Kintsugi celebrates the brokenness in the pottery and rejoices in what the brokenness brought about—something more wonderful than before. The brokenness is not hidden or ignored. The gold reveals the richness that now glows from the pottery.

The prophet Isaiah said to God, "We are the clay, you are the potter; we are all the work of your hand" (Isaiah 64:8). We are each molded by God like pieces of pottery. Because of sin, we are cracked and broken, but God in his mercy joins the pieces of our brokenness back together in glorious fashion through the suffering and death of his Son Jesus, whose blood repairs our brokenness. His glorious resurrection seals our status as forgiven and whole children of God. In Christ, we are new creations (see 2 Corinthians 5:17). Our brokenness, now repaired, proclaims to the world the brilliant work of God in our lives.

FOR REFLECTION

What cracks in your life have led to greater glory in Christ?

Butterflies

Therefore, if anyone is in Christ, he is a new creation. The old has passed away; behold, the new has come. **2 CORINTHIANS 5:17**

The butterfly is truly a "new creation" that comes out of a cocoon (a tomb of sorts) after a period of time. What once was a scrawny, worm-like creature crawling on the ground is now a colorful, beautiful, glorious creation that can fly to great heights.

What a wonderful picture of what happened through the resurrection of Christ! We who were once lowly, sinful creatures are made new. We are filled with Christ's life, soaring in service for him in this life and, on the Last Day, flying to be with him in heaven.

This is the wonderful news of Easter. Because Christ went through this transformation from death on the cross, to three days in the tomb, to resurrection life, we, too, will rise from death and the grave to a glorious eternal life. Every day is now an Easter Day, a day to celebrate that we are now God's "butterflies," flitting from place to place to spread the good news that Jesus is alive, and because he lives, we will live with him forever.

FOR REFLECTION

When have you felt as free as a butterfly?

Signs of the Resurrection

The church that I attend has a sign language interpreter who communicates the worship to hearing impaired parishioners. I am very often drawn into and moved by her signing. I noticed that the sign for "He is risen" is two fingers pointing downward, then floated down and placed upon the palm of the other hand, a very literal and visual interpretation of that event. I could see in that sign the miracle of the resurrection and the humanity of Christ in the depiction of his body.

What other "signs" of the resurrection of Christ do we see in the world? I think of flowers budding from seemingly barren ground, butterflies emerging from very rough-looking cocoons and wobbly baby birds that take wing and fly.

We know that when our Lord returns on the Last Day, our bodies, too, will be raised to new life. As it says in Romans 8:11: "He who raised Christ from the dead will also give life to your mortal bodies because of his Spirit who lives in you." What a comfort to know that Christ's resurrection means our resurrection. His new life means new life for us, forever with him!

FOR REFLECTION

When have your hands signaled your connection to Jesus?

Ombré

Ombré, meaning "shaded" in French, is the blending and gradation of one color hue to another, usually from dark to light. It is an increasingly popular technique in fashion, hair color, nail art and baking.

The concept of *ombré* has religious overtones, if you will. When we think of the death and resurrection of our Lord, for instance, it is an *ombré* moment as Christ moves from the darkness of death on Good Friday to the light of life on Easter. Mary Magdalene came to the tomb on Easter morning "while it was still dark" (John 20:1), but the light of the sun gradually rose as she began to realize that the Son of God had risen.

The concept can also be applied to our experience of sanctification, as we gradually become more like Christ. As the Bible says, "And we all, with unveiled face, beholding the glory of the Lord, are being transformed into the same image from one degree of glory to another" (2 Corinthians 3:18). Our lives become more beautiful with our Savior with each passing day.

FOR REFLECTION

When have you felt like you were going from darkness to light?

Pivotal Questions

Many pivotal questions were asked at significant moments in the story of salvation. Why is that? Consider these:

> *"Why do you look for the living among the dead?"* **LUKE 24:5 (NIV®)**

> *"Why are you troubled, and why do doubts rise in your minds?"* **LUKE 24:38 (NIV®)**

> *"Why do you stand here looking into the sky?"* **ACTS 1:11 (NIV®)**

At the first Easter, the women were sure that Jesus was dead, but the question reveals the good news that Jesus is alive. In the upper room, the disciples were frightened by the sudden appearance of Jesus, but Christ's question assures them that they do not need to be afraid. At the mount of the Ascension, the disciples were at a loss to understand what they had just seen, but the angels' question explains exactly what had happened.

Through these straightforward questions in the story of salvation, we can see that God has his plan all worked out!

FOR REFLECTION

What pivotal questions have you wrestled with?

CHRIST-FILLED MOMENTS

Hesed

The Hebrew word *hesed* is translated as "lovingkindness" in most Bibles, but a word so rich in meaning cannot be adequately described in English. Other translations use the words "covenant," "faithfulness" and "steadfast love." It is love that is literally beyond words.

The word reveals God's character. He loves us beyond measure, beyond what we can even comprehend. It is a love that can never be matched fully in human terms. It is a love that will stop at nothing to care for us and protect us.

Hesed is most fully realized in the incarnation of Jesus. Jesus is *hesed* in the flesh. And he went to the greatest lengths of love to save us. He went to the cross to suffer and die and sacrifice his life for us all. "Greater love has no one than this, that someone lay down his life for his friends" (John 15:13). Then God's *hesed* went beyond even the grave when he raised Jesus from the dead on Easter morning.

Christ is alive and living in us; God's *hesed* transforms us to live a new life of divinely inspired love and compassion for others. We love as we have been loved, with our whole selves, giving our all for one another in the name of the God of *hesed*.

FOR REFLECTION

When have you encountered the deep richness of God's love?

Strength of My Life

The LORD is my light and my salvation;
whom shall I fear? The LORD is the strength of my life;
of whom shall I be afraid? **PSALM 27:1 (KJV)**

My confirmation verse was Psalm 27:1. I chose it because I liked the description of the Lord as "my light and my salvation." A friend showed me a plaque he received as a farewell gift when he left one congregation to serve as a musician in another. It reads: "The Lord is the strength of my life." He has put it on the wall next to his front door so he sees it whenever he heads out anywhere.

What a nice reminder that is for us all as we leave our homes—the Lord is the strength of our lives. We need his strength. He is the core, the center, the driving force that carries us forward in our lives.

When we exercise, we are supposed to "work the core," the center of our bodies around the torso, because when the core is strong, the rest of our body becomes stronger. The strength of the Lord makes our entire selves, soul and body, strong because he is strong.

Think about the strength God gives today. Draw upon that core strength, and say with the psalmist, "Of whom shall I be afraid?"

FOR REFLECTION

How does God give you strength throughout the day?

Moon Rocks

When Neil Armstrong brought back moon rocks from the Apollo 11 mission in 1969, the rocks were distributed to all 50 states, but many of the mementos vanished. Saddened by this development, rock hunter Joseph Gutheinz sought out the missing treasures. He successfully located all the states' rocks, except for two, New Jersey and Delaware.

While some of the rocks were stolen, Gutheinz discovered that 40 states did not record where they put the moon rocks. They simply lost track of them. Something similar can happen with the treasure of our faith in Christ, received by the power of the Holy Spirit through baptism.

Our precious faith can be ignored, or buried under work assignments or personal hobbies. Perhaps we have lost touch with some fellow believers.

In one of Jesus' parables, a woman searched for a lost coin. She was determined to look for the coin until she found it and was overjoyed when she discovered it. Our attitude should be the same as we re-embrace our faith and our fellow followers of Christ. Set aside some time to search for special friends in the faith and reconnect.

Never let the Word of God or the bonds you have with others disappear from your life!

FOR REFLECTION

Who would you like to reconnect with first?

Rebuilder

There are many television shows about rebuilding, restoring or redecorating homes. We are fascinated by the way carpenters and designers reimagine a space or home. At the reveal, homeowners respond to the finished product with exclamations of delight.

I recently heard the song "Rebuilder" by the Christian group Carrollton. It celebrates our God as the greatest rebuilder of all, not of our homes but of our lives. When we are in bad shape and in need of repair because of sin, doubt or waywardness, he rebuilds us on the foundation of his goodness and grace, his blessing and love. The end result is a new creation because of the work of his Son, the carpenter, who followed through with the rebuilding of all believers by going to the cross for our forgiveness. The old is gone; the new has come (see 2 Corinthians 5:17). There is great excitement in the reveal of our redesigned lives: "There is joy before the angels of God over one sinner who repents" (Luke 15:10).

No matter the condition in which we find ourselves, God can rebuild us and the results will be glorious: "We are his workmanship, created in Christ Jesus for good works, which God prepared beforehand, that we should walk in them" (Ephesians 2:10). What a wonderful craftsman we have!

FOR REFLECTION

What needs the most rebuilding in you?

When You Pass Through the Waters

When you pass through the waters, I will be with you;
and through the rivers, they shall not overwhelm you;
when you walk through fire you shall not be burned,
and the flame shall not consume you. For I am the LORD
your God, the Holy One of Israel ...   ISAIAH 43:2-3

In these verses, God speaks to the Israelites, assuring them that, whatever came their way, he would bring them through.

Watching the aftermaths of hurricanes that have hit Florida and Texas in recent years, we can see firsthand the power of water. You cannot ignore the forceful flood waters that threaten you. You must endure the danger. There are many stories of people who were rescued by boat or helicopter from the rising waters. Those rescue operations are a metaphor for the way our God rescues us from the rising waters of troubles at work, home or school. We must pass through them, yet God assures us that he will lift us out. God will not let us be overwhelmed or consumed by any obstacle in our path. Why? Because he is with us, and he is the Lord. He is the one to whom we cling in the midst of strife.

FOR REFLECTION

What troubled waters do you need rescuing from?

All That Matters

Dear friends, now we are children of God, and what we will be has not yet been made known. But we know that when Christ appears, we shall be like him, for we shall see him as he is. **1 JOHN 3:2 (NIV®)**

When I lead Bible class in my church, there are times when the only answer I have to a difficult question is: "We will have to ask Jesus that one when he returns in glory." We as humans are an inquisitive bunch. We want to know and understand everything right away. But there are simply some things that we will never know this side of heaven.

What we need to remember is not so much what we do not know, but what we do know:

- We are children of God.

- Christ will appear to take us home to heaven.

- We are dearly loved by our Savior.

- We are forgiven and saved from all our sins through the suffering and death of Christ.

In the end, the questions about what we don't know do not really matter, because what we do know is all that matters.

FOR REFLECTION

What helps you focus on what matters?

Gentleness

Let your gentleness be evident to all. The Lord is near.
PHILIPPIANS 4:5 (NIV®)

Paul wants to make sure that the gentleness of the Philippian congregation is evident to all. Why? Because the Lord is near. We want to see our gentle ways as we wait for the Lord's return.

In a world in which people are often hostile toward one another, our gentleness can stand out. We only need to look to our Lord Jesus to understand gentleness. He said, "I am gentle and humble in heart" (Matthew 11:29, NIV®). He took little children into his arms and blessed them (see Mark 10:16). He spoke gently even of those who crucified him, saying, "Father, forgive them, for they do not know what they are doing" (Luke 23:34, NIV®).

We can be humble in our approach to people, embrace children and care for those around us. We can be gentle, forgiving those who have hurt us and recognizing that we are all sinful and in need of the grace and mercy found only in the cross. Even when we witness to others of the hope we have in Christ, we are to do so "with gentleness and respect" (1 Peter 3:15). We need to be comforting, not overbearing, in sharing our faith. Be gentle in your ways today, with the help of God.

FOR REFLECTION

How is gentleness a blessing and not a detriment?

Genealogies

Websites like ancestry.com and 23andme.com let people trace their genealogies. I have learned that although my aunt was born a Zimmermann (a German name), her heritage comes far more from Great Britain than Germany.

Scripture carefully traces the lineage of Jesus. Matthew tracks the generations from Abraham to Jesus, highlighting Jesus' connection to the line of King David. Luke follows Jesus' ancestry all the way back to Adam. The genealogy from Abraham to Jesus confirms God's promise to Abraham, "In you all the families of the earth shall be blessed" (Genesis 12:3). The genealogy traced to Adam reveals the fulfillment of God's promise of a Savior in Genesis 3:15, when he said to the tempting serpent, "And I will put enmity between you and the woman, and between your offspring and hers; he will crush your head, and you will strike his heel" (NIV®).

By faith we have been grafted into the family of God by the blood Christ shed on the cross for the forgiveness of sins. God's promises of old apply to us as well. "If you belong to Christ, then you are Abraham's seed, and heirs according to the promise" (Galatians 3:29, NIV®). Each Sunday is a family reunion with brothers and sisters in Christ. Enjoy being part of this holy heritage!

FOR REFLECTION

What does it mean to you to be in God's family?

Attractors

On a community garden tour, I learned that certain plants are called attractors because they attract butterflies. Not just any plant attracts any butterfly. Black-eyed Susans are known attractors of Monarch butterflies, asters attract Painted Lady butterflies and zinnias draw Swallowtails.

In our Christian witness, are we living "attractors" who draw others to learn about our faith by the way we live? Jesus said, "Let your light shine before others, so that they may see your good works and give glory to your Father who is in heaven" (Matthew 5:16). How can we attract others? Our response to difficult circumstances with hope and confidence in Christ may attract others. They may be curious about a response that runs counter to the expectations of secular society.

Like specific plants for specific butterflies, we are sent by God to be present to particular people. You might be the attractor for someone who desperately needs to know that he or she is forgiven through Jesus.

Watch for people who search for meaning and direction. Attract them to the Good News of Jesus by praying with them, reading Scripture together or inviting them to church.

Like flowers and butterflies, Christian witness is a beautiful thing.

FOR REFLECTION

Whom can you attract with the Gospel?

Plein Air

Plein air is a French expression that means "open air" and is a practice of painting in which artists work outdoors. Artists travel around the country, capturing moments with paint on canvas. In *plein air* competitions, artists submit work of scenes painted in a limited time period. Artists paint in thunderstorms, in 100-degree heat and in 30-degree cold. *Plein air* painting keeps artists from dwelling too much on the small details.

This art practice parallels what we must do as Christians in this world as we "paint the picture" of our salvation in Jesus for others. We may be called on the spot to witness to others and have no time to prepare. In that moment we must speak from our heart and soul. The Holy Spirit helps us in this task: "The Holy Spirit will teach you in that very hour what you ought to say" (Luke 12:12). The conditions may not be perfect, but the message is just as beautiful no matter where you declare it. Like the *plein air* artists, you do not need to worry about the minor details or the exact words. God will make a masterpiece of your on-the-spot "word pictures" of forgiveness and eternal life found in Jesus Christ.

FOR REFLECTION

What picture can you paint of God's love today?

Recalculating

Recalculating. We all have experienced hearing that word at one time or another when we are using our GPS and go a different way than the app has mapped out. Though we have gone "off-course," our GPS finds a new way to get us back on track.

The idea of recalculating recalls for me the work of our Good Shepherd in our lives. "All we like sheep have gone astray; we have turned—every one—to his own way" (Isaiah 53:6). When we have gone our own way, our Good Shepherd comes and finds us. Our Good Shepherd tells us, "What do you think? If a man has a hundred sheep, and one of them has gone astray, does he not leave the ninety-nine on the mountains and go in search of the one that went astray? And if he finds it, truly, I say to you, he rejoices over it more than over the ninety-nine that never went astray" (Matthew 18:11-13). Jesus is our divine GPS. He did the recalculating for us by going to the cross to save us from our sins and put us on the path to everlasting life.

Let the Good Shepherd lead you on the path he has set for you.

FOR REFLECTION

When have you gone off-course in your faith?

Blooming in the Dark

On a garden tour, I learned about a plant called the moonflower. This is a flower that only blooms at night under the light of the moon. I began thinking about the way some of our gravest and most fearful moments hit us at night. How many times do we wake in the night in a panic, worried about an approaching deadline or an unresolved issue? When that nighttime terror comes again, think of the moonflower. Like the moonflower blooming, Christ comes to us at night with the comfort of his Word: "In this world you will have trouble. But take heart! I have overcome the world" (John 16:33, NIV®).

Like the (potentially) romantic moonflower, our heavenly Father comes to us in love: "I have loved you with an everlasting love; therefore I have continued my faithfulness to you" (Jeremiah 31:3). The moonflower stays open until sunrise, just as the Holy Spirit stays with us until Jesus returns on the Last Day to take us to himself forever. Like the fragrant moonflower, what sweet joy our triune God offers us, day and night, as he carries us through life into eternity.

FOR REFLECTION

What has blossomed in your life, even in dark times?

The Graduation Verse

This is what I have come to call "the graduation verse": "For I know the plans I have for you, declares the LORD, plans for welfare and not for evil, to give you a future and a hope" (Jeremiah 29:11). It is an inspiring verse that comforts those who send children, nieces, nephews and other loved ones off on their adventures beyond particular school walls.

In this verse, God says that he *knows* the plans he has for each of us. He is not "thinking about it" or "undecided" or "exploring various options," sentiments we may hear from graduates. God *knows* what he has in mind for each of our graduates. If God has a plan for each person, then *we* know that that plan is a good one, one for our welfare and our ultimate benefit.

What does that plan look like? It has a future. It is a plan that is going somewhere. It will have direction, a goal, a mission—and it has hope. God's plan keeps driving, keeps moving, keeps striving. Hope means that there is meaning and purpose in what God has in store. God will be a part of that plan every step of the way, because only he is our hope.

FOR REFLECTION

How do you stay on track with God's plan for you?

Take His Yoke

*Take my yoke upon you, and learn from me, for I am gentle
and lowly in heart, and you will find rest for your souls.
For my yoke is easy, and my burden is light.* MATTHEW 11:29-30

An actual yoke does not look easy or light, but in the hands
of our Master, it is.

Oxen wear a yoke so they can be controlled by the farmer.
The oxen must follow the guidance and direction of the
farmer. This keeps the oxen on the right path. With Christ as
our guide, we learn how to maneuver through the treacher-
ous portions of life, as he did on the way to the cross for our
salvation.

One translation of these verses says that our Master's yoke
"fits well." It is not a "one size fits all" sort of approach. The
weight of the mission placed upon us by our Lord is custom
designed for us. So being yoked to our Savior is not something
against which we struggle, but something to treasure and use
to celebrate the gifts God has given to us.

Our Savior promises to be gentle. His gentle hands on the
reins make our work for him manageable and pleasing to him
and to ourselves. In this light, what a privilege it is to take on
his yoke.

FOR REFLECTION

What helps you to give the reins of your life over to Christ?

CHRIST-FILLED MOMENTS

Stay Strong

I am feeling weak. But you, O God, are strong. And you give strength to your people. As you gave strength to Abraham, so keep me strong in my faith. As you gave strength to Moses, so keep me strong over the long haul. And as you gave strength to David, so keep me strong in the face of giant obstacles. Amen.

This prayer I wrote helps me to remember that I am not alone when I feel weak. Abraham in his old age (and Sarah in her old age) were promised a son, but it didn't happen right away. God gave Abraham strength to have faith in the promise, and Isaac was born in God's time. That same strength from God keeps me strong in my faith.

Moses felt weak at the prospect of leading the Israelites out of slavery, saying he didn't speak well. But God gave him strength to lead his people and guide them to the Promised Land. That same strength from God keeps me patient and confident in the journeys through my life.

David was no match to the giant Goliath. But God gave David strength to fling a stone from his slingshot and fell that foe. God gives me strength against a giant foe, the devil, so that I can defeat his temptations with the Word.

FOR REFLECTION

How do you stay strong in weak moments?

Walking on Water

When the disciples were in a boat during a storm, Jesus came to them, walking on the water. They thought he was a ghost, but Jesus said, "It is I!" (Matthew 14:27). Sometimes we may think of Jesus as some sort of spirit floating around in the air, but as Jesus himself revealed, he has flesh and blood. He is fully human and fully divine.

When Peter asked to come out onto the water, Jesus said, "Come" (Matthew 14:29). For a time, Peter walked on the water through Christ's power. This happened to real flesh-and-blood people. Then Peter was distracted by the waves and wind and started to sink. Focusing on the power of Christ in our lives keeps us moving forward. When we look away from him, things start to go downhill. Yet even as Peter was sinking, Jesus reached out his hand to save Peter. When things go downhill, Christ is there to pull us to himself.

Jesus said to Peter, "O you of little faith" (Matthew 14:31). Our weakness in faith can pull us away from him. We pray that the Holy Spirit will keep us close and connected to our Lord. Jesus came to earth for all who are enveloped in the storms of life. Jesus' stilling of the storm foreshadowed the stilling of the storms of sin that surround us.

FOR REFLECTION

What storms can Jesus help you out of?

Those Things That Are Lost

The parables of Luke 15 tell of things and people that are lost. The woman searching for the lost coin is like our God, who looks for all who are lost and living apart from him. When he finds us, the angels celebrate that the lost has been found. What a joy it is to be celebrated and treasured!

In another parable, one sheep among 100 is lost. The shepherd leaves the 99 to find the lost sheep. The shepherd cares for each and every sheep, but he leaves the majority to rescue the minority. Once he finds the lost sheep, he carries it on his shoulders, returning in victory. Whenever we get off track in our lives, we have the assurance that our Savior will come and get us back on track with him.

The parable of the lost son captures what it means, in human terms, to be lost and then found by God. The young son asks his father for his inheritance and then spends the money in reckless and wasteful living. When the son realizes how wasteful he has been, he seeks to return to his father's house. When we realize how reckless we have been with God's gifts, we turn to God in repentance. When the lost son returns to his father, his father welcomes him with a party. When we return to God, he forgives us our sins, and we will be his honored guests at heaven's victory feast!

FOR REFLECTION

When have you been lost and then found by God?

The Rich Young Man

A rich young man asked Jesus, "What must I do to inherit eternal life?" (Mark 10:17). Jesus answered with a list of the commandments. The young man said of the commandments, "All these I have kept since my youth" (Mark 10:20). "You lack one thing," Jesus said. "Go, sell all that you have and give to the poor" (Mark 10:21). The young man walked away sad because he had many possessions and was not willing to give them up. Jesus said to his disciples, "It is easier for a camel to go through the eye of a needle than for a rich person to enter the kingdom of God" (Mark 10:25).

We are very attached to possessions, things that can become our gods. Consider our possessions—homes, clothing, cars, furniture, appliances, phones and other electronic devices. Can we live without them? Some things we could easily give up, but we would have a hard time giving up other things. Why? These things define who we are in this world. Things bring us comfort and confidence, but things are not who we are. Those things will all pass away. We need to cling instead to our Savior, Jesus. His love lasts forever. He defines who we are—children of God and brothers and sisters in Christ. Jesus is our treasure!

FOR REFLECTION

What reminds you that you are rich in Christ?

50

Legacy Narratives

Legacy narratives are stories of the events of your lifetime that you wish to pass on to future generations. This is becoming popular now as people begin to sense that younger generations are not as well aware of their pasts as generations before them were, and there is a driving urge to leave something of meaning and value to others.

As Christians, we can jump on the legacy narratives bandwagon by relating stories of the way Christ has brought us through struggles and difficulties in our lives and how he has shown us God's will and way for us, often when we were not even looking in that direction.

The Gospels themselves are a legacy narrative. They tell the story of how Christ came into the lives of four different people: Matthew, Mark, Luke and John. Each of them wanted future generations to know about their Lord and Savior: "Now Jesus did many other signs in the presence of the disciples, which are not written in this book; but these are written so that you may believe that Jesus is the Christ, the Son of God, and that by believing you may have life in his name" (John 20:30-31).

FOR REFLECTION

What would you want to include in your legacy narrative?

An Anchor

We have this hope as an anchor for the soul,
firm and secure. **HEBREWS 6:19 (NIV®)**

Recently I went boating with some friends on a nearby lake. In a quiet cove, a heavy anchor kept the boat steady while we swam and floated on rafts. Even though the boat was anchored, it still moved around because of prevailing winds, waves from other boats and currents from the lake. I had always imagined that once a boat was anchored, it stayed put. That is not the case.

Our hope in Christ is an anchor for the soul. Though the anchor is firm and secure, we who are tethered to it are not always still. We are pushed around by doubts, fears and the opinions of those who say that God does not matter or that Christianity has become passé. It is not always easy up here on the surface. The waters of life can be rough.

We may be tossed about, but with hope and faith in Christ, we know that our God will never let us go adrift. He keeps us firmly planted in the depths of his love so we remain on course in our faith. We are safe in his forgiveness and grace. That is our hope. That is our anchor. That is our salvation.

FOR REFLECTION

How can you stay still when anchored to Christ?

A Zacchaeus Moment

I tend to sympathize with Zacchaeus. He was interested in Jesus, but he had trouble seeing him in the crowd. Zacchaeus was resourceful, so he climbed a tree. He didn't really want to be seen himself, but Jesus pointed him out. Jesus made it clear that he wanted to talk to him and spend time with him and even go to his house. Zacchaeus must have been mortified. I know I would have been. Like Zacchaeus, I am curious about things but like to stay in the background. But Jesus brought Zacchaeus to the forefront. Why? Jesus explained: "For the Son of Man came to seek and to save the lost" (Luke 19:10).

Have you had a "Zacchaeus moment"? A time when it became clear that Jesus came for you personally and that he wanted a relationship with you? I remember a time when I, as a young boy, was holding the processional cross in church. I was physically lifting high the cross of Christ who came to save me and I started weeping. Maybe for you it was just a feeling you had or it may have been an event. But in any case, there comes a time when Jesus finds you and your world is never the same again. Marvel at that moment today.

FOR REFLECTION

How do you see yourself in Zacchaeus?

Positive Proximity

There's a term in urban planning getting a lot of traction these days: *positive proximity.* The term refers to ways in which neighbors in a community work together in a positive manner to achieve a worthy goal. The driving force behind positive proximity is that it can cause a chain reaction of random acts of kindness in a community. One person waving hello can lead to a conversation about working together on a project to keep the sidewalks clean, which can lead to increased foot traffic to shops and storefronts.

It is important in positive proximity to be open and available. Being out and about in front of your church or home can help neighbors see that you care about the place you are in and that you care about the community. Jesus was positive proximity in action: "Jesus went through all the towns and villages, teaching in their synagogues, proclaiming the good news of the kingdom and healing every disease and sickness" (Matthew 9:35, NIV®).

Our role as Christians, too, to be the hands and feet of Christ out in the world, not simply existing inside the dwelling places of God in brick and mortar. Have a positive impact on a next-door neighbor today.

FOR REFLECTION

What specific activities can bring you closer to God and others?

Trajectory of Engagement

The trajectory of engagement is the movement from online communication to offline relationships. This concept is having a large impact on Christians today. Engagement on social media may be a good start in personal relations, but it cannot be the end result. We, as Christians, know that faith engagement must at some point be person-to-person. The trajectory must go beyond technology to faith-based living. Many conversations I have with people in the Church are through text messages, which are great for sharing a quick story or an encouraging word but cannot replace being together in person. The online and the offline communication must work in tandem for a deeper connection.

What would it have been like if Jesus had lived on earth during this time of social media? Would he point us to the parable of the Good Samaritan? Would we be like the priest and the Levite who walked by the person in need because we were texting our friends?

It's time for us to look up from our phones and view social media not as an end in itself, but as a beginning, a doorway into more meaningful real-life personal relationships with our brothers and sisters in Christ.

FOR REFLECTION

When have you moved from online to offline engagement?

The Peace of God

As a traveler toured Spain, the tour guide cautioned to beware of thieves. In the middle of a cathedral, the traveler was startled by a woman who approached, speaking with a hand outstretched. The traveler remembered the warning and shrank back. Only later did the traveler realize that the woman was saying, "*La paz de Dios,*" the peace of God. She was sharing the peace.

Do I hesitate to share the peace of God with others during the passing of the peace in church because of the way people look or how they approach me or how I am feeling? There are multiple barriers that we throw in our own paths that prevent us from sharing the peace of God. We need to stop shrinking back and, instead, reach out to others.

The peace of God may surprise us and present itself when we are not looking for it. We may be so caught up in fears about one thing or another that we miss God saying, "Peace be with you!" through a word from a passerby, a comment on the TV or a billboard on the highway. God may use creative and unusual ways to spread his peace to us. We just need to watch and listen for them.

FOR REFLECTION

How can you be more present in sharing the peace?

CHRIST-FILLED MOMENTS

The Baader-Meinhof Phenomenon

After you buy a car, you seem to see that make and model of car again and again on the road. That experience is called the Baader-Meinhof Phenomenon. Scientists have found that our brains like patterns, so our brains are constantly searching for things that are alike, a characteristic which is helpful for memory. When repetition happens, the brain elevates the information because the repeated instances make up the beginnings of a sequence. Then something called the recency effect kicks in, which is a cognitive bias that inflates the importance of recent stimuli or observations. This increases the chances of being more aware of the subject if we encounter it again in the near future.

While we may be able to chalk up these coincidences and patterns to brain function, I have no doubt that often the Holy Spirit may have something to do with it. How many times have we noticed someone or something on our drive to work or our walk at lunch that we had not noticed before ... and then we noticed that person or thing again? As Christians, we might consider that the Holy Spirit is using such experiences to direct us to a situation in which we may need to act—and certainly a situation over which we need to pray!

FOR REFLECTION

When has the Holy Spirit pointed someone out to you?

The Healing Power

Jesus' healing of the paralyzed man in Luke 5 applies to our lives today. Consider the four friends who carried their friend to healing. Who has brought you close to Jesus? Thank God for them today.

The way to Jesus was unusual. The friends carrying the paralyzed man could not go through the door to find Jesus. The crowds were too big, so they lowered their friend through the roof. Thank God for helping you to see new ways to Jesus and giving you the power to follow the unusual paths he may put before you as you receive help from our Savior.

Jesus' interaction with the paralyzed man was rather unexpected as well. When the paralyzed man was finally placed before Jesus, the first thing Jesus did was forgive the man's sins. When you go through trials in your life, remember that it is the blessing of forgiveness in Christ that is needed more than any physical need.

Then Jesus told the paralyzed man, "Go!" The man could not do that before—go out on his own two feet and walk. Jesus tells you, "Go!" Go in the power of the Spirit and follow the path marked out for you by God. "Go!" means that you are healed and ready to move forward in Christ.

FOR REFLECTION

When have you experienced the healing power of Christ?

The Good Samaritan

In Jesus' parable of the Good Samaritan, the man who was beaten and left for dead must have thought no one would help him. He must have been surprised when the person who stopped to help him was a Samaritan—from a group of people who were more or less his people's enemies. When you were in distress, were you helped by someone you did not know? Give thanks to God for help from unexpected people and places.

The priest and the Levite who walked by the injured man represent those of us who are busy. We are not willing to help those in need. We may say we are too tired or our schedules are too tight or others could take care of the problem. Ask God to open your eyes to the plight of others. Give of your time and resources.

The Good Samaritan made the effort to stop and help the injured man. He was not afraid of any differences he had with the man or the animosity people may have felt toward him because of his heritage. In his parable, Jesus teaches us to go the extra mile to care for those who cross our path and to give of what we have to bless the lives of those who are poor in spirit and in worldly goods.

FOR REFLECTION

When have you been called to be a Good Samaritan?

The Feeding of the 5,000

The feeding of the 5,000 is a good example of the generosity of Christ. Taking five loaves and two fish and turning them into enough food to feed 5,000 shows us how Christ takes the little we have and makes it more than enough.

In John 6, we discover that the five loaves and two fish come from one little boy. This reminds us that our own generosity can be increased by the generosity of Christ to supply the needs of others. In Matthew 14, the disciples are pessimistic about what can be done to feed so many people, but Jesus turns the situation back to the disciples, saying, "You give them something to eat" (Matthew 14:16). The miracle happens through his power in their hands.

Mark 6 says the disciples had the 5,000 sit down in groups of one hundreds and fifties. There must have been organization in the arrangement of the crowd and the distribution of the food. You can imagine the conversations among the people as they sat down together in a way that would best facilitate the sharing of the food. Bonds of fellowship were begun and built through this process. Being a small part of a big assembly is vital to Christ's overall plan, so play your part well.

FOR REFLECTION

What little things in your life has God used to bring help?

The Faith of the Centurion

When Jesus encountered the centurion, the officer knew what Jesus could do for him. He asked for healing for his sick servant. The centurion understood what it meant to be the leader over others. "I say to one, 'Go,' and he goes, and to another, 'Come,' and he comes" (Matthew 8:9). He knew the power of a leader and the obedience of a servant under his command. The centurion knew that Jesus was such a leader. The centurion knew that the Savior had authority over all things, including illness. The Lord healed the centurion's servant and said, "With no one in Israel have I found such faith" (Matthew 8:10). This was a shocking statement because the centurion was not a member of the tribes of Israel. The centurion was a Roman, a member of the empire that ruled over Israel itself.

We, too, live as foreigners in a foreign land. We are citizens of the earth, but we are also citizens of God's kingdom. We will find among us people like the centurion who honor and trust the Savior, even though they seem to be part of a group that does not believe in him. Never turn away from anyone who is expressing faith in Jesus, no matter what their background or how they may be viewed by others. "Whoever is not against you is for you," Jesus said (Luke 9:50, NRSV).

FOR REFLECTION

How can your faith be more like the centurion's?

Ten Lepers

There were 10 men with leprosy who met Jesus on the road, begging for mercy that they might be healed (see Luke 17:11-19). How bold it was to plead for mercy from Jesus! If we are sick and in need of help and healing, we should not be too proud or afraid to ask Jesus for help.

Jesus told the men to go and show themselves to the priests. The men did as they were told. On their way they were made clean. Jesus had healed them. We can imagine the men cheering and celebrating and running to their homes to share what had happened to them with relatives and friends. But one man returned to Jesus and gave thanks for the miracle of healing, the blessing Christ had given him.

To the shock of everyone, the returning leper was a Samaritan, not one of the people of Israel. The Samaritan knew what it felt like to be ostracized and what it meant to be recognized and healed by Jesus. This Samaritan bowed before Jesus, showing his humility. He knew he did not deserve this goodness from Jesus. We, too, can show humility and thanksgiving for the goodness and mercy shown to us in Christ's help and healing of our illnesses and our sins.

FOR REFLECTION

What have been your reactions when you have been healed?

Sunburn

I was recently sunburned across my legs and torso after lying on a raft in the water for several hours, even though I had worn sunscreen. I continued to feel the sharp sensation of the sunburn under my clothing at work and home. I realized that unless I told somebody, no one would know the burning I was feeling.

The disciples on the road to Emmaus said to one another after they saw Jesus, "Did not our hearts burn within us while he talked to us on the road, while he opened to us the Scriptures?" (Luke 24:32). They did not hide the burning sensation they felt in Jesus' presence. "That same hour they got up and returned to Jerusalem; and they found the eleven and their companions gathered together ... Then they told what had happened on the road" (Luke 24:33-35, NRSV).

When has your heart burned within you, spiritually speaking? While reading the Bible? During prayer? When singing in church? Tell someone about your experience. The Holy Spirit's power burns within us as we tell others about our encounters with Jesus. Explain how Jesus opened your eyes and what it means to be a disciple of Christ. Explain the joy you feel because your Savior is alive in the world. Let your burning heart for the Lord be revealed!

FOR REFLECTION

With whom do you want to share the Good News?

Out of the Tombs

Jesus healed a man who had not been in his right mind and was living naked out by the tombs, cutting himself (see Luke 8:27-36). After his healing, people now saw the man dressed, speaking plainly and in his right mind.

Those who are naked are not protected and not covered by the robe of righteousness from Christ. They are open to the elements and to the evils of the world. The man was cutting himself, which reveals his dishonor toward his body and his disrespect toward himself. The man was not speaking plainly; he was not fully in the Word and did not understand the Word of God spoken to him. The devil took hold of the mind God had given him. Not being plain in speech makes it clear that God was not in control of the man's thoughts.

The healed man was an object lesson in and of himself. This man's newfound ability to speak, his clothed body, his clear mind and his end to cutting made people realize that Jesus was at work. The man himself spread the word that Jesus had transformed him and that Jesus was his Savior. People came to believe in Jesus because of this man and his healing.

FOR REFLECTION

What stories of adversity help you to persevere?

Perfectly Carved

Visiting Mt. Rushmore in South Dakota, I was amazed by the perfect carving of the faces of George Washington, Thomas Jefferson, Teddy Roosevelt and Abraham Lincoln. One small slip of the carver's hand and the monument would have been ruined.

The psalmist said, "For you formed my inward parts; you knitted me together in my mother's womb. I praise you, for I am fearfully and wonderfully made. Wonderful are your works; my soul knows it very well. My frame was not hidden from you, when I was being made in secret, intricately woven in the depths of the earth" (Psalm 139:13-15). God shaped us, knit and wove us into the people he wanted us to be. St, Paul writes, "We are God's masterpiece" (Ephesians 2:10, NLT). Each of us is beautifully designed by God, but sometimes we have a hard time reminding ourselves of that fact, especially when sin plunges us into feelings of low self-esteem or perceived unworthiness.

God, our Creator, takes great delight in each one of us. He wants us to celebrate what he has brought to life in us. In his skilled hands, our bodies and souls, faces and features were fashioned in his image to reflect his great love and tender care to the world.

FOR REFLECTION

What has God fashioned you to do or to be?

Camping

My family often went camping. My dad would ask me to spread the tarp for the "add-a-room" that was attached to the camper. Ropes and stakes kept the enclosure steady: "Enlarge the place of your tent, and let the curtains of your habitations be stretched out; do not hold back; lengthen your cords and strengthen your stakes" (Isaiah 54:2).

It sounds like God wants us to apply the principles of camping to our lives. He wants us to spread out where we dwell, not limiting ourselves to one small area. He wants us to include people. He wants us to reach out beyond ourselves by firmly putting down stakes in his salvation. Others will see that we are solidly established in the rich soil of his Word. St. Paul was a tentmaker by trade (see Acts 18:3). Through the Spirit, Paul built dwelling places for God in the hearts of people. He laid down the groundwork of faith that allowed people to weather the storms of life. He covered them with the Good News that Jesus suffered and died for their sake.

Every earthly house we have lived in will one day pass away, but our spiritual tents with God will last forever. Our souls and bodies will be housed with him eternally under the canopy of his love.

FOR REFLECTION

Whom would you like to see living under God's tent?

One Thing Needful

Mary and Martha of Bethany were good friends of Jesus and they had him over for dinner one night. Many people may have wanted to have Jesus over for dinner at the time, but Jesus chose to share a meal with Mary and Martha. Think of the meals you have shared with friends, the good times, the laughter, the conversations and good food. Mary and Martha must have looked forward to all of that with Jesus.

But think, too, of how nervous you might be if you knew Jesus was coming to dinner at your house. You would want everything to be just right. You would want to make sure the house was clean and the meal was cooked to perfection. This is what Martha was thinking in her preparations for Jesus' arrival. Jesus gently scolded Martha, and he does the same for us. He does not want us to be worried and nervous about anything, let alone many things. Our task is to break out of sinful habits and live as Christ's disciples should.

Mary apparently did what Jesus desired. She sat at his feet and listened to him, and Jesus praised her for it. He said Mary chose the one thing needful (see Luke 10:42). Jesus wants us to choose what is needful as well.

FOR REFLECTION

When has worry overpowered your focus on Jesus?

Day Lilies

One spring day, orange day lilies started popping up in my neighborhood. I saw them in other parts of St. Louis, and then they appeared in my own backyard. I learned from my mom that they are perennials that bloom once a year. They sure live up to the saying: "Bloom where you are planted." They are blooming everywhere, and they are blooming brightly.

I have been on the lookout for them and have seen them along the highway, in ditches, in alleyways and next to dumpsters as well as in the front and back yards of homes and in flowerbeds alongside buildings. No matter where I see them, I can't help but smile.

How can we be like day lilies in our Christian lives? We can be a bright spot in a person's day when that person wasn't expecting it. We can show up in rough places with the Good News of the Gospel. We can draw attention to the Lord's beautiful displays as we go about our usual routines at work or at home. Be a "day lily" this day and every day.

FOR REFLECTION

Where has God planted you to bloom today?

Gravel Roads

On a trip to South Dakota, I saw the Badlands and Mount Rushmore, the Corn Palace and Wall Drug, buffalo in Custer State Park and monolithic stones surrounding Sylvan Lake. I used the Google Map app on my phone to get around. The voice directing me would sometimes announce a turn moments before an intersection. Often the app was silent for hundreds of miles because I was on the same road the whole time. Most difficult were the gravel roads in Nebraska recommended by the app on the way home. *This can't be. There must be some mistake.* But then I would zoom out on my phone and see that the gravel road was the fastest way to get to my destination. So I bumped along in my increasingly dusty car and arrived home safely.

The car is still a little dusty, but the Google app did not steer me wrong. Life sometimes takes us down gravel roads that don't seem right, perhaps an illness, a death in the family or a rough spot in a relationship. "This can't be right," we say. But stepping back, we can see that it was all part of a bigger road trip laid out for us. God is like that Google app voice saying, "Go straight." He will take you safely home.

FOR REFLECTION

What gravel roads have you traveled on toward God's goal?

A Boat in the Storm

The disciples were with Jesus on a boat when a storm blew in. The disciples turned immediately to Jesus, but Jesus was asleep. "Save us," they pleaded (Matthew 8:25). But Jesus calmly said, "O you of little faith," and stilled the wind and the waves and the rain (Matthew 8:26). The disciples were astonished: "What sort of man is this, that even winds and sea obey him?" (Matthew 8:27).

We are often at peace in the boat of our lives; we know that Jesus is with us. Then when a storm comes along and rocks the boat, we panic. We rouse Jesus from slumber, begging him to save us. Jesus, without much fanfare, stills the storm in our lives and renews our faith. Peace returns to our hearts, and Jesus remains to dwell with us. The boat of our lives sails until it reaches the shores of heaven, where we will dwell in blessed union with Christ and our fellow believers, giving praise to God, who welcomes us to paradise.

When Jesus tells the wind and waves, "Be still," he is telling us, too, to be still. We should not be anxious or panic when things start going wrong. Jesus is always with us and he will bring his peace to our lives.

FOR REFLECTION

When has the boat of your life been stilled by Christ?

CHRIST-FILLED MOMENTS

Our Refuge

God is our refuge and strength, a very
present help in trouble. PSALM 46:1

It seems as if this verse was made for us today. During the thick of the pandemic we took refuge in our homes for extended periods of time to stay safe and protected from the virus, just as we take refuge in our God, who keeps us safe and protected from evil and danger is this world.

We continue to do all we can to keep ourselves strong health-wise, wearing masks when needed, washing our hands regularly and standing six feet from each other in long lines. But our greatest strength comes from our God, who cleanses us from all sin and keeps us strong in our faith. He surrounds us with his power against all that would seek to weaken us.

God's help is very present. It is not something old or forgotten. His help is real and up-to-date. We do not need to worry that somehow God does not understand what today's troubles are like. He is well aware of all that we are going through, and he is able and willing to help. God has things under control, and we are in his care.

FOR REFLECTION

What are you seeking refuge from today?

Thirsty?

If anyone thirsts, let him come to me and drink.   JOHN 7:37

For what do we thirst? Are we thirsting for Jesus? Or are we thirsting for wealth or for a human relationship? Do we thirst for happiness or for a good job? Do we want popularity or fame?

We hear again and again from doctors and other health experts that we should drink eight glasses of water a day. But do we? I for one find myself drinking more soda than bottled water, more sports drinks than tap water. We know what is best for us, but we don't always drink what we should.

To come to Christ and drink means to be in prayer more often than we are on the internet. It means reading his Word in the Bible more often than watching TV. It means being filled with his Spirit more often than stuffing our faces with food.

So come to Christ and drink. Be thirsty for time with him. Crave his presence with you. Be soothed by his messages of hope and blessing, peace and love. Let his words wash over you and be poured into you over and over again each and every day.

FOR REFLECTION

What helps you to thirst more for Christ?

Now I See

It seems that no matter who you are and no matter what your eyesight has been in the past, once you reach or near a certain age, you will need glasses. I have worn glasses nearly my entire life, but when I was getting into middle age, I discovered I needed new glasses and different glasses for various tasks.

This change in my eyesight needs reminded me of the following words from Scripture: "One thing I do know, that though I was blind, now I see" (John 9:25). This was said by the blind man who was healed by Jesus.

We have blind spots in our lives that change with age and that Jesus helps us to see. Like a new pair of glasses, Jesus helps us to see better the needs of older adults that we didn't notice when we were younger. He opens our eyes to opportunities to serve that we had not seen before. Once blind to God at work in the world, we now see his hand reaching out to make things happen, to his glory, through the lens of Jesus Christ. No matter what your age or eyesight situation, let Jesus give you the vision to see what he can do through you.

FOR REFLECTION

Who is one person you see who needs your assistance?

150 Devotions for Your Walk of Faith

Slides

My aunt and uncle recently gave me 46 carousels of slides from my grandfather's trips to Europe and the Holy Land. "But how will I see them?" I wondered. I was also given an old projector. "But where will I show the slides?" My aunt and uncle also brought a screen. The experience reminded me of these verses:

> How, then, can they call on the one they have not believed in? And how can they believe in the one of whom they have not heard? And how can they hear without someone preaching to them? And how can anyone preach unless they are sent? As it is written: "How beautiful are the feet of those who bring good news!" **ROMANS 10:14-15 (NIV®)**

We are like a projector shining a light on the Word of God so that people see and understand it. The Word of God is reflected on us, so people will see how Christ impacts the blank slate of our lives. The story of our faith is revealed as it is captured in words and actions illuminated by Christ.

My grandpa's journeys were shown in his slides. Our journey of faith is shown in our lives. Shine the light on the One who is the Light of the World. Then people will see. And people will believe.

FOR REFLECTION

What has helped you to share about Jesus?

Biking

I learned a few things when I started biking again. The first thing is that you cannot get right back to where you once were. You have to ease your way in. I found that I was not going as fast as I once was and that it took more energy. When I got home, I was sore. I also remembered that it is not best to bike in the baking sun of midday. On weeks when I rode a little later in the day, it was not as warm and there was a breeze along the way.

Finally, I discovered that even the slightest incline makes a bike ride more difficult. My body started objecting with aches and pains as soon as I went uphill. Turning around and going downhill felt like a dream after that.

These experiences mirror the Christian life. Sometimes it takes time to get it right, to hit our stride as Christ's disciples. We need to be patient so we do not become discouraged as we learn to follow Christ and look for opportunities to witness. The path is long and God will never give up on us. We should not give up on ourselves.

FOR REFLECTION

What struggles have you faced on your ride of faith?

Renewal

Thank you, loving Father, for restoring our joy in you through the birth of your Son, Jesus. May his presence among us resurrect in us a new sense of peace and liveliness in living our lives refreshed by our Savior's forgiveness and renewal. Amen.

The prayer above is something that I wrote for Christmas, so let's enjoy a little Christmas now by giving this prayer some thought.

During any time of the year, it is nice to remember that Jesus brings renewal and restoration. There is always a chance to start over again with Jesus. He is reborn in us each and every day, and any time we feel down and out, Jesus can lift us up and into his arms.

The resurrection is a reminder that with Jesus alive in us, we have nothing to fear and we can be at peace. Living in him should be lively and active, something that moves us forward in our faith. From the manger to the empty grave, our Jesus has moved forward for us. It's our turn now to move forward for him with acts of forgiveness, love and service.

FOR REFLECTION

What needs renewal in your life?

In the World, Not of It

They are not of the world, just as I am not of the world.
JOHN 17:16

As Christians, we must remind ourselves daily that we are in the world but not of it. We are easily drawn into things of this world (money, clothes, food, homes, jobs) and forget to pay attention to things not of this world (heaven, salvation, God).

How can we pay attention to what is important? Look to Christ and mirror what he did and said while on this earth. Jesus said: "For life is more than food, and the body more than clothing" (Luke 12:23). Christ talked to people about the kingdom of heaven and the ways of God. He wanted people to know more about what is unseen than what is seen. St. Paul tells us, "So we fix our eyes not on what is seen, but on what is unseen, since what is seen is temporary, but what is unseen is eternal" (2 Corinthians 4:18, NIV®).

That is the heart of the matter. The world and everything in it will one day pass away, but our life in Christ will last forever. It is time, therefore, for us to release our grip on earthly things and hang on more tightly to the everlasting things.

FOR REFLECTION

What do you look forward to in the world to come?

Sunflowers

In late summer one year, I heard about a large sunflower field a fair distance from my house. I wanted to get there to see the sunflowers for myself but I kept putting it off. Finally I decided to make the trek, only to find I was too late. The sunflowers had lost their color and were all drooping forlornly. I took a picture of myself with the sad-looking sunflowers anyway.

As I drove away from the field that once was so full of life, it made me think about the fact that we as Christians often need to act right away when an opportunity to share our faith presents itself or the chance for a beautiful result may slip away. Don't get so caught up in yourself and your activities that you miss an opening to share God's love in Jesus.

The experience also made me remember the words of Isaiah who said, "The grass withers, the flower fades, but the word of our God will stand forever" (Isaiah 40:8). The fading sunflowers actually became a comforting reminder that the Word of the Lord will never fade away. The Word is a bright burst of sunshine in our lives every day. Opening the Bible can be like opening a forever-flourishing flower. Let the words bloom within you.

FOR REFLECTION

What needs your attention right now?

Food Trucks

Food trucks are becoming popular these days, with people lining up to eat in business areas, parks and neighborhoods. Wherever the wheels can go, the food can be offered.

Food trucks show us what we as Christians can provide to people who do not know Christ. St. Paul said, "I have become all things to all people so that by all possible means I might save some. I do all this for the sake of the gospel, that I may share in its blessings" (1 Corinthians 9:22-23, NIV®). We, like food trucks, can serve different things to different people in the name of the Lord. We can supply sympathy to one who is sad or give strength to one who is weak. We can dish up Scripture to those who want to inwardly digest the Word. We don't need to fixate on one type of outreach or a single Bible verse. We can adjust and be a blessing in various ways to different people.

As Christ's disciples, we can be quick to get on the road and go where God's Word is needed most, aware of Scriptures that will satisfy the spiritual palates of those we encounter. In the end, may all those we serve "taste and see that the LORD is good" (Psalm 34:8).

FOR REFLECTION

What acts of service have you engaged in?

Gardening

In late summer my parents had extra tomatoes and zucchini from their garden to give away to friends and neighbors. The abundant harvest led to acts of generosity and sharing. Those who received the garden's bounty had fresh and healthy produce and enjoyed the time spent catching up with my parents.

We share the fruit of the Spirit with family, friends and neighbors. The Holy Spirit has given us an overabundance of his fruit, so we can freely give to others our love, joy, peace, patience, kindness, goodness, faithfulness, gentleness and self-control. Sharing with others brings happiness and an increase of faith. They may grow in their relationships with us, and the fruit brings health to their souls.

How can you be like a gardener, giving of God's bountiful crop? Make a visit to a loved one, relate a story that touches the heart, sit with someone waiting at the hospital or supply a meal to someone who is overwhelmed with work and family life. We can be good gardeners for God, sharing the Holy Spirit's fruit. Keep growth in the Spirit going!

FOR REFLECTION

What growth in faith have you recognized in yourself?

Running on Empty

I often see how far my car can go when it is on E. Not too smart, I know. I eventually succumb to reason and fill the tank. How often do we do the same thing when it comes to our energy level? We can find ourselves many times at the end of the day completely wiped out.

God does not want us running on empty. He wants to fill us with the power of the Holy Spirit. He wants us to recharge our batteries with the strength only he can provide.

After long days of teaching and healing, Jesus took time to be filled with strength from above. He "would withdraw to desolate places and pray" (Luke 5:16). Where do you go to be renewed in the Lord? Maybe it is during prayer or reading Scripture at the end of the day or on a long walk after dinner. Whatever fills your spiritual life, keep doing it. Take advantage of the opportunities to be with the Lord. The apostle Paul writes, "Let us not grow weary of doing good, for in due season we will reap, if we do not give up" (Galatians 6:9). Times of restoration keep the weariness at bay. Keep your tank full as God continues to do great things through you.

FOR REFLECTION

What helps you most to stay filled with faith?

Love One Another

On the night Jesus was betrayed, he gave a new commandment: "Love one another: just as I have loved you, you also are to love one another" (John 13:34). This is no ordinary love; it is a love grounded in what Jesus was about to do on the cross. It is a love that is selfless, sacrificial, deep, complete and life-saving. Loving others as Jesus loves us is not something that comes naturally to us. We want to love others only to please ourselves and satisfy our own needs. Jesus shows us a love that puts others first and ourselves last. We find in Jesus a way of love that reaches outward and expects nothing in return.

"God shows his love for us in that while we were still sinners, Christ died for us" (Romans 5:8). We were enemies of God when Christ died for us. We did not deserve his love, yet he loved us by giving his all for us. Jesus tells us, "Love your enemies and pray for those who persecute you" (Matthew 5:44). It is Jesus' kind of love that we can exhibit in our lives. It is a love that goes against conventional wisdom. Yet it is the love that we have experienced and a love that we (and Christ) want others to experience through us.

FOR REFLECTION

How can you show Jesus' kind of love today?

The Body of Christ

For the body does not consist of one member but of many.
If the foot should say, "Because I am not a hand, I do not
belong to the body," that would not make it any less a part
of the body. And if the ear should say, "Because I am not
an eye, I do not belong to the body," that would not make
it any less a part of the body. **1 CORINTHIANS 12:14-16**

This passage sounds ludicrous and basic at the same time. We cannot imagine a part of the body wanting a promotion or exercising total domination. Simple biology requires parts of the body to stay where they are and do what they were created to do. Yet so often that is not what we in the body of Christ do. We seek from God a different role to play. We ask, "Why did you make me this way?" "Why aren't my talents being used?" "Why are other people getting more attention than I am?"

"I made you this way for a reason," God might say. "I put you in this place because you are greatly needed here. This is not a competition." All parts are working for the Lord and all things are done to his glory. Rejoice that you are part of Christ's body!

FOR REFLECTION

How have you become more accepting of yourself in Christ?

Christ of Our Lives

On a trip to Eureka Springs, Arkansas, I saw the "Christ of the Ozarks," a large statue of Jesus with arms outstretched. It is similar to the Christ the Redeemer statue in Buenos Aires, but it has its own look that tells you that you are in the Ozarks.

How does Christ look to you? What are the prominent features of "Christ of Mark Zimmermann"? When I think of Christ, I think of his loving eyes. I picture his arms reaching forward to embrace me. I ponder his smile upon me. Take a few moments today to consider how Christ looks to you. How do you see his face? How is he standing before you? Perhaps take some time to draw your concept of Christ.

Each of us may experience Christ in different ways, but the attributes of Christ that remain the same are his everlasting love and care, his forgiveness and grace. Christ himself will never change. Thanks be to God!

FOR REFLECTION

What stands out to you about Christ?

Crossword Puzzles

I recently began doing crossword puzzles. I had not done them before because I felt they were too difficult for me. But doing puzzles on a regular basis has helped me to get better at them and made them easier to do. Now I look forward to my "crossword time" and enjoy the experience, especially when I "get" a hard word that opens the door to more words in the puzzle.

We may experience the Word of God in a similar way. At first we may avoid it and think it is too difficult for us. But then when we read the Bible regularly, it becomes easier to do. It feels good when it becomes part of our routine. When we do "get" a word or passage, story or parable from Scripture through the power of the Holy Spirit, we are excited and enlightened and our minds are opened to other messages in God's Word.

As with crossword puzzles, all the words of Scripture are connected to each other, and we become more connected to God as we see the interrelationship of his communications to us.

FOR REFLECTION

What helps you grow in your understanding of Scripture?

Energy Boost

One of my vices is to drink Pepsi or Coke every morning. I know it may not be the best choice, but it gives me an energy boost to get me going in the day. Others drink coffee, tea or sports drinks for a lift to start their tasks. The Lord gives us an energy boost like no drink on earth can. Consider these enlivening words of Scripture:

> The joy of the LORD your strength. **NEHEMIAH 8:10**

> For whatever was written in former days was written for our instruction, that through endurance and through the encouragement of the Scriptures we might have hope. **ROMANS 15:4**

> Be strong and courageous. Do not be frightened, and do not be dismayed, for the LORD your God is with you wherever you go. **JOSHUA 1:9**

The joy of the Lord, the Scriptures, having hope, knowing that God is with you and being renewed as we wait for him—all of these give us the energy boost we need. As you indulge in your morning energy drink, look to Scripture to energize your faith. The Word brings you everlasting liveliness in God.

FOR REFLECTION

What energizes you the most in your Christian life?

Weeds

When I finally did some yardwork, I found that weeds had been thriving. I cut down the weeds to help the good plants flourish and make my yard look good. But the roots of the weeds remained, although unseen. So, eventually I will be cutting down weeds again. The experience reminds me of this parable Jesus told:

> The servants of the master of the house came and said to him, "Master, did you not sow good seed in your field? How then does it have weeds?" He said to them, "An enemy has done this." So the servants said to him, "Then do you want us to go and gather them?" But he said, "No, lest in gathering the weeds you root up the wheat along with them. Let both grow together until the harvest, and at harvest time I will tell the reapers, 'Gather the weeds first and bind them in bundles to be burned, but gather the wheat into my barn.'" **MATTHEW 13:27-30**

The weeds and good plants will grow together. We repent and root out the weeds of sin in our lives, but we will still suffer the evil that the devil sows in the world. When Jesus returns, all evil will be destroyed and we, his harvest, will be gathered into his presence.

FOR REFLECTION

What weeds of the world give you the most trouble?

Binary Stars

Binary stars are two stars that orbit around a common center of mass and are gravitationally bound to each other. We who are lights of the world for Christ are tied to other lights in our Christian "solar system." Our light for Christ may be linked to the ones who first shone their light of Christ on us, to other "lights" in our families or those who were in confirmation, Sunday school or Bible classes with us.

Knowing that we have lights that are attached to us helps us to shine brighter, confident in their encouragement and support. When our lights grow dim because of some darkness we have experienced, our "light" partners will brighten our light and life again with their love and care.

We are bound together by the light of Christ, and in him the bond between tandem lights grows stronger. Savor and value the unique bonds with other "lights" with whom God has blessed you in the vast constellation of his people.

FOR REFLECTION

Who are your binary stars?

Photography

In a college photography class I had, we took and developed our own pictures in the photo lab. We learned about different lenses and f-stops. In the dark room, we rolled our film onto a reel and used photo paper in a chemical solution to reveal the image. As an amateur photographer in today's digital world, I do not need to worry about these steps anymore. All I have to do is hold up my smartphone, hit the camera icon and tap the red button to take a picture to send immediately to my friends and family.

Like the changes in photography, we may sometimes have trouble keeping up with changes in our Christian lives. There is "the way we used to do it" and the way "everybody is doing it" now.

The old or new way may be neither bad nor good, better or worse. It just is. We can adjust to changes regardless of the way we may have done things before. The new ways may not feel comfortable at first, but in the end they are doing what the old ways have always done—bringing the Word of God to the people who need to hear it. Watch as a picture of our Savior, Jesus Christ, is revealed.

FOR REFLECTION

What are some changes in your Christian life?

In the Background

In these days of Zoom meetings, we get to see where people actually live. One time in a Zoom meeting, a coworker of mine noticed a book on a bookshelf behind me that he also had. Wall hangings, knickknacks and comfy-looking chairs in other homes have caught my eye.

These glimpses into people's lives lead me to ask, "What do people notice behind us (literally and figuratively) that reveal our connection to Christ and our life of faith?" It might be a cross on the wall, a Scripture verse on a plaque or a Bible set on a bedside table. But our faith is also revealed in setting aside a time for prayer and reading Scripture daily, things we do "behind the scenes," so to speak, that enliven our face and demeanor with others. Our spiritual background can have a great impact on what goes on in the foreground of our lives. People are watching, and we have a great opportunity to show others the reason for the hope we have (see 1 Peter 3:15). Do not be afraid to share "what is behind you," as you witness to Christ.

FOR REFLECTION

How have you helped to build faith in others?

Trivia Night

And no longer shall each one teach his neighbor and each
his brother, saying, "Know the LORD," for they shall all know me,
from the least of them to the greatest, declares the LORD. For I
will forgive their iniquity, and I will remember their sin no more.

JEREMIAH 31:34

Trivia night is a popular pastime. In person and now online, people gather in teams as an announcer reads questions in various categories. Teams answer and at the end of all the rounds, the team with the most answers right is declared the winner. I am always amazed by what people know. One woman on my online team knew that MMA stood for Mixed Martial Arts, though she never watched the sport. Another person knew that the group Baha Men sang, "Who Let the Dogs Out." How did she know that?

"How do we know that the Lord is God?" We just know, not because of anything we have done, but because the Holy Spirit has put that knowledge into our hearts, souls and minds. This is not trivial knowledge; it is essential. Knowing the Lord means knowing we are forgiven and that we are loved and remembered by him forever. It's not just good to know, but everlastingly life-affirming to know.

FOR REFLECTION

How can you share what you know about Christ?

Videos

I was recently asked to read devotions on a video. I learned a lot in the process. I learned that it is not easy to set up my smartphone just right to capture my image for the recording. The background had to look pleasing, without any distracting stray items, I found. It was also important to read through the words on the page a few times before recording.

Those video lessons can also be applied to prayer. It is good for us to spend time preparing for a moment of prayer, adjusting ourselves to speak to God in a clear and direct way. We also pray the best when we rid our surroundings of all distractions and hindrances to our time with God. The words we pray silently or aloud become easier to pray the more often we utter them.

By the last video I produced, I had a better handle on what to do to make it go smoothly. Staying in constant prayer can have the same effect. Prayer becomes more natural in our spiritual lives. So keep the prayers coming. God is happy to hear them.

FOR REFLECTION

What can you do to improve your prayer life?

CHRIST-FILLED MOMENTS

Through a Mirror Dimly

St. Paul writes, "For now we see in a mirror dimly, but then face to face. Now I know in part; then I shall know fully, even as I have been fully known" (1 Corinthians 13:12). Mirrors in Bible times were made of highly polished metal, with limited reflecting ability. That is why St. Paul refers to seeing dimly through a mirror. That is the only way you could see yourself, as a hazy outline.

Today we see too much of ourselves, with our floor-length mirrors, bathroom mirrors and mirrors in hallways and elevators. Doctors can see inside of us with X-rays, ultrasounds, CT scans and MRIs. We may think that we know ourselves inside and out.

But there is still so much we do not know about ourselves and about our place in this world. We are also "in the dark" about the experience of eternal life. But the good news is that one day we will see the face of God before our eyes. We will know all about the world to come. When we pass from this world to the next, we will view like never before the love, mercy and grace that God lavished upon us through Christ, who came to earth to wipe the haze of sin away from our lives forever.

FOR REFLECTION

Why is it good to know that God knows you fully?

Invisible Ink

When I was young and our family went on a trip, my mom would often buy us "invisible ink" books. With a special yellow pen you could uncover the answers to questions, find interesting animals or see characters of a story.

The idea of invisible ink is a reminder to us that God has a story to tell us right beneath the surface of our lives. We are sons and daughters of our parents, but beneath the surface, we know we are part of a greater family, the family of God. We are citizens of the country where we dwell, but hidden beneath that is our citizenship in the kingdom of God. We see ourselves as students, parents, workers, teachers, children, friends and many other daily roles, but beneath the surface, Christ lives within us. He is guiding our thoughts, words and deeds, so that when people see us, they see Christ. We don't need a special pen or pencil to make any of this happen. It happens through the Holy Spirit, who helps us to see with new eyes the divine story that is being revealed to us and in us.

FOR REFLECTION

How are you reminded of what is beneath the surface?

Updates

I don't know about you, but I get tired of always getting messages on my computer to update to the next operating system or the latest version of a particular program that I use. It is a struggle: Do I "move up" or keep things as they are?

In our Christian lives, the answer is always to update, to move forward, to begin anew. That is why we have confession and absolution every time we worship. Through God's grace and mercy, we need to be upgraded from sinful to forgiven people of God again and again. Staying "where we are" spiritually on any given day only keeps us in our sins and separated from our source of renewal in God through Christ. Spiritual updating also means returning to the Word of God on a regular basis.

Life in the Christian faith is all about newness and growing and not giving up. So don't be afraid to keep updating your life of faith with prayer, confession, devotions and Bible readings. Growing closer and closer to Christ in more and more ways brings blessings upon blessings. Let the updates abound.

FOR REFLECTION

What updates of faith do you need the most help with?

Scrapbooks

I have scrapbooks in my attic and look at them occasionally, but not as much as I thought I would. The art of scrapbooking has faded in this era of electronic pictures as well, so future generations may not have as meticulous a record of a person's life in any particular year.

We have another book that tells us everything we need to know about our background and about the events that we should remember. The Bible is the Church's scrapbook. It reminds us of what God's people experienced through thousands of years of history. It tells us about creation, sin, the journeys through the wilderness, the triumphs in battle and the defeats suffered. It highlights the life of our greatest family member, Jesus, who went to the cross for our salvation on Good Friday and rose for us on Easter Sunday to bring us everlasting life.

The Bible should never be a book we store away in a dusty attic. It should be a book that is always at our fingertips and open for us to explore frequently. The Bible reminds us of who we are as children of God and what we should treasure most: that through Christ our names are written in the Book of Life forever. Happy reading!

FOR REFLECTION

What parts of the Church's scrapbook do you enjoy the most?

Gift Bags

Many presents now, for birthdays and other special occasions, are found in gift bags, not wrapping paper. Why is that so? Here is what I came up with:

They are easier to wrap—no scissors, tape and measuring.

They are easier for the recipient to unwrap—no picking at corners and trying to undo tape.

They are easier for the recipient to carry home, using the built-in handles.

What does this have to do with Christian living? We often make sharing our God-given gifts with others more difficult. We bind up our love with the tape of selfishness and hostility. We often make it hard to break through the barriers we put in place to block our kindness and care. We as Christians should be drawn to the "gift bag" approach of sharing with others. Our hearts should be open and easy to access. Our gift-giving should be something that comes naturally and without much trouble to receive. Our gifts should be something that the recipients can carry home to enjoy and even share with others, just as people re-use gift bags for presents to others. The gift-giving multiplies, to effortlessly give and receive God's gifts of love.

FOR REFLECTION

How is your gift-giving going?

Pivot

One of the buzzwords these days is the word *pivot*. It is used to describe how we change and adjust our ways, maybe on a moment's notice, to get a task completed. In recent times, many have pivoted by working from home instead of in the office and using Zoom for meetings.

Jesus pivoted in his ministry, preaching from a boat when the crowds got too large, meeting with Nicodemus at night and talking up to Zacchaeus in a tree. St. Paul spoke of pivoting: "I have learned in whatever situation I am to be content. I know how to be brought low, and I know how to abound. In any and every circumstance, I have learned the secret of facing plenty and hunger, abundance and need" (Philippians 4:11-12). Paul learned to be content in the place to which he pivoted.

God calls us to be content when circumstances require us to worship online, when it is recommended that we wear masks in church or when we have to have Bible studies on Zoom. God is at work in every pivot and adjustment. We are fed by the Word in every way it comes to us. We have opportunities every day to pivot to spread the Word of God. All we need to do is be ready for those moments and be content with the experiences, however unorthodox they may seem.

FOR REFLECTION

When have you had to pivot recently?

CHRIST-FILLED MOMENTS

Church in the Woods

In Eureka Springs, Arkansas, I visited Thorncrown Chapel, a beautiful work of architecture tucked in the woods. When you enter the space, a greeter asks you to sit down in the pews and quietly listen to music and take pictures.

Seated, you look up at the soaring ceiling of wood beams crisscrossing one another. To the right and left, you can see the trees and foliage directly outside the windows. Your eyes turn toward the side lights shaped into a cross.

The chapel reinforces the fact that God created the wonders of nature. The beauty he designed is seen in every plant and creature. The chapel reminds us that we, too, are part of God's creation, formed in his image to tend and care for the earth. Tending and caring for the earth is an act of worship, a task we should not take lightly. We should honor the earth and celebrate the joy it brings to us. We should sing praises as we work to preserve the world around us and take the time to marvel at the Creator's handiwork.

Yet as the chapel architecture reminds us, it is the cross of Christ that should crisscross every angle as we view the earth around us. It is that cross that makes all of life beautiful beyond measure.

FOR REFLECTION

When have you felt most in touch with God's creation?

First and Last

*If anyone would be first, he must be last of
all and servant of all.* MARK 9:35

Who is usually thought to be first? It might be wealthy people
or those who are famous. Who would be last? It might be
people who are poor or homeless or those who are meek and
shy.

Jesus tells his disciples that those who want to be first will
be last of all. In the kingdom of God, it doesn't matter how rich
or famous you may be. If wealth and fame are most important
to you, then you will be last in the kingdom of God because
you do not put God first.

Those who are poor in the things of this world are first
in the kingdom of God because God looks out for the poor
and cares about those who are humble. God chose a stutterer
named Moses to lead the Israelites out of Egypt. God chose
the little shepherd boy David to be king. God chose Mary,
a simple young girl, to be the mother of Jesus. Throughout
Scripture, God chooses the last person you would expect to
be the first person he picks. So put yourself last that you might
be first in the eyes of God. You will be blessed.

FOR REFLECTION

What does being last for the Lord
look like for you?

CHRIST-FILLED MOMENTS

The Language of God

In the story of the Tower of Babel, we read that all people on earth spoke the same language. In their arrogance, they decided to start building a massive tower that would reach to the heavens. But God confused their language, humbling them (see Genesis 11:7). The building of the tower stopped and the people scattered to various parts of the world.

The story of the Tower of Babel has some vital applications to our circumstances today. So many groups of people in the world are speaking the same language of hate and discord no matter what their native languages may be. They are building "towers" of influence and power that negatively influence the advance of the kingdom of God in the world.

Into the growing spread of divisive language, God enters and breaks up the network of hostile talk to replace it with a language of love. The result is discourse grounded in Christ and not in ourselves. It is a communication that is built on giving and not taking away. The language of love transcends all other languages and fosters forgiveness over domination. God wants there to be no more babbling about what we dislike in one another but, instead, an understanding that we work better together when we speak first in love.

FOR REFLECTION

How do you speak the language of love in your life today?

I See You

A common catch phrase in pop culture these days is the comment "I see you." It is used as a way of simply saying, "I recognize your recent accomplishment." But it has recently taken on the connotation of "I understand where you are coming from" or "I realize what you are going through" and even "I notice you as a potential love interest."

Jesus often "sees" people where they are. "Jesus saw Nathanael coming toward him and said of him, 'Behold, an Israelite indeed, in whom there is no deceit!' Nathanael said to him, 'How do you know me?' Jesus answered him, 'Before Philip called you, when you were under the fig tree, I saw you.' Nathanael answered him, 'Rabbi, you are the Son of God! You are the King of Israel!'" (John 1:47-49). Jesus sees Nathanael as a good disciple even before Nathanael knows it. Nathanael responds with faith and gratitude. Jesus sees each of us the same way. He knows the potential within us to serve him even before we do. We are excited to help others see what Jesus sees in each of us—his devoted followers.

FOR REFLECTION

What do you think Jesus sees in you?

Stress Ball

I have a stress ball at my desk. I confess that I give it a squeeze or two once in a while when things get tough. It relieves the tension for a time and gives me a sense of calm for a moment. But the problem is that the stress comes back and I cannot be squeezing a stress ball every minute of the day. That is not a productive use of my time. That is why it is important to turn to Scripture for lasting stress relief. Consider these verses:

> *Come to me, all who labor and are heavy laden,*
> *and I will give you rest.* **MATTHEW 11:28**

> *Peace I leave with you; my peace I give*
> *to you. Not as the world gives do I give*
> *to you. Let not your hearts be troubled,*
> *neither let them be afraid.* **JOHN 14:27**

> *Take heart; I have overcome the world.* **JOHN 16:33**

> *And behold, I am with you always,*
> *to the end of the age.* **MATTHEW 28:20**

These words from Jesus are more effective than any stress ball in calming our troubled hearts and minds. Let the Word be your ultimate stress reliever in difficult times and at all times.

FOR REFLECTION

When are you most in need of stress relief?

Fragrance

But thanks be to God, who in Christ always leads us in triumphal procession, and through us spreads the fragrance of the knowledge of him everywhere. For we are the aroma of Christ to God among those who are being saved and among those who are perishing ... **2 CORINTHIANS 2:14-15**

After being with someone who is wearing perfume, you may still smell that perfume after the person leaves. That is what we are to be with others as we spread the Gospel: a sweet perfume that lingers. Like sweet perfume, our words about Christ can permeate the air with the aroma of grace and forgiveness and love. Our witness is like the loving actions of Mary of Bethany, who anointed the feet of Jesus with expensive ointment and wiped his feet with her hair. "The house was filled with the fragrance of the perfume," we read in Scripture (John 12:3).

What we say about Jesus and our worship of him can have a lasting impact on those around us, even if we don't think so at the time. Our words matter, and our faith in Jesus has a lingering effect. People remember what Jesus means to us. We pray that they may come to breathe in the scent of Christ's constant presence in their own lives.

FOR REFLECTION

When have you truly sensed Jesus' presence?

No Longer Elementary

*But now that you have come to know God, or rather to be
known by God, how can you turn back again to the weak
and worthless elementary principles of the world, whose
slaves you want to be once more? You observe days and
months and seasons and years!* **GALATIANS 4:9-10**

The ways of the world are weak and worthless and elementary, while the ways of God are strong and certain and deep. We do not live to gain the favor of God, as was done with false gods. But we live to love him in response to what Christ has done for us on the cross. Our observances of the special days of the Church Year are ways of honoring our God, not appeasing him as some sort of requirement.

We are often prone to falling back into following the false gods of our day, things like fortune, fame, popularity, possessions, entertainment and job advancement. We should instead follow the desires of our God and act according to his will, in ways that are no longer elementary, but divinely inspired. God gives us peace that the world cannot give, hope that is an anchor for the soul and grace by which we are saved. Everything else can be turned aside.

FOR REFLECTION

What false gods do you tend to be most influenced by?

Empty Nets

As we all know, many of the disciples were fishermen. Scripture reveals that the job was difficult, referring to two specific times when the fishermen ended up with empty nets:

> And Simon answered, "Master, we toiled
> all night and took nothing! But at your
> word I will let down the nets." LUKE 5:5

> Simon Peter said to them, "I am going fishing."
> They said to him, "We will go with you."
> They went out and got into the boat, but
> that night they caught nothing. JOHN 21:3

How often do we experience the pain of "empty nets"? With Jesus in our lives, we need to remember that empty nets are never the end of the story with our Savior. Any disappointment we may experience along the way cannot compare to the overflowing gifts Jesus grants to us in his time. Jesus sees us in our distress and will provide us in the right way with more than we need to carry on. Our work through hardships only sweetens our moments when we realize that it is Christ alone who fills our empty nets, supplying us, as he supplied the disciples, with everything necessary to serve and follow him.

FOR REFLECTION

What have been your empty nets?

Human Object Lesson

An argument arose among them as to which of them was the greatest. But Jesus, knowing the reasoning of their hearts, took a child and put him by his side and said to them, "Whoever receives this child in my name receives me, and whoever receives me receives him who sent me. For he who is least among you all is the one who is great." **LUKE 9:46-48**

This teaching of Jesus would not have had the impact that it did were it not for the living, breathing child before them. Jesus continues to teach lessons to all the world through living, breathing people—you and me. We, too, are Jesus' human object lessons. What does he teach through us? We stand before the world as examples of sinners, for we have done what is evil in the sight of God. And we stand before the world as real-life illustrations of what it means to be loved and forgiven by Christ through his cross. We are called to live out our response to that grace through words and actions that are loving and caring, hopeful and helpful, for all to see.

FOR REFLECTION

How have you been a human object lesson today?

The Carpenter's Son

Is not this the carpenter's son? MATTHEW 13:55

There is something very telling about the people in his home-town calling Jesus the carpenter's son. It suggests a familiarity with him. It also connects Jesus to a trade. It is assumed that Jesus was trained by Joseph in the art of carpentry and that this is the path that Jesus will follow in his work life.

That is why the townsfolk are so astonished when they hear "their" Jesus speaking so eloquently and with such wisdom and authority on spiritual matters in the synagogue. This was not the Jesus they expected. Jesus was not the regular kid from down the block anymore. He had a story to tell of God's plan and a people to save. This was not what the community had in mind for him.

Or was it? It is no mistake that Jesus was born in a wooden manger crafted by hand to hold straw, and it is no coincidence that Jesus was nailed to a wooden cross. Christ's connection to wood and carpentry bookends his perfect life on earth for our redemption. It is no surprise that Christ continues to fashion a life for us that is designed to serve his purpose.

FOR REFLECTION

What has Christ the Carpenter crafted you to be?

Tornadoes

Meteorologist Tetsuya "Ted" Fujita was dubbed "Mr. Tornado" because of his knowledge of and devotion to the study of tornadoes. He developed the F-scale that is currently used to describe the severity of a tornado. He discovered the existence of downbursts and microbursts, which changed the ways that weather was predicted and air travel was conducted, ultimately saving thousands of lives. His findings came about through his meticulous recording of the aftermaths of severe storms. What he saw at the end of these events told a story of what had happened before to cause such destruction.

This man's story shows us a picture of what we should be doing in our lives as Christ's followers. We, much like Mr. Tornado, are called to assess the damage of sin in our lives and determine what can be done about it. We have seen homes wrecked, families broken, people injured or killed because of "tornadoes" of sin that have ripped through the lives of so many. But the more we understand sin in the world, the better we are able to prepare for it. Sin seeks to destroy us, but God seeks to lift us up. Focus on him.

FOR REFLECTION

How has Christ helped you through "tornadoes" of sin?

A Desolate Place

He would withdraw to desolate places and pray. LUKE 5:16

The Bible tells us that Jesus would get away to desolate places in order to pray. It sounds a little counterintuitive. Shouldn't Jesus be out with the people and doing miracles all the time? That is what many people expected of him. But Jesus was fully human as well as fully divine. He needed time away to regroup and be inspired and filled up again, just like we do.

It is all right to take a break, to get away from it all, to be by yourself for a while to talk to God and be recharged for service in Jesus' name. We can't do everything, and there are only so many hours in the day. We need to be realistic and practical about what can and cannot get done in a day. The Spirit will guide us to what needs to be done first and to what can wait until later. To stop and care for yourself and your own needs is called self-care. It is not being selfish. It is being kind to yourself when you are in low gear, and it is allowing yourself the chance to be renewed by the Lord in your mission and purpose.

FOR REFLECTION

Where do you go to take a break to be with God?

Stars and Sand

One of my favorite verses in Scripture is God's promise to Abraham that his descendants will be as many as the stars in the sky and the sand on the seashore (see Genesis 22:17). And this was before Abraham's son Isaac was even born. Abraham had to trust God's word.

I have looked up to the sky at night and marveled at the multitude of stars I can see. I have also seen thousands of grains of sand slip through my fingers and toes along seemingly endless expanses of seashore. God paired stars with sand: stars from above and sand from the earth. God is in charge of both the heavens and the earth; no part of creation is beyond his reach and his handiwork.

The message of stars and sand is one of blessing—abundant blessing. We are in the hands of God, who richly provides for us, far surpassing our imagination or comprehension. We, like Abraham, can only put our faith in God and trust that he will care for us in beautiful and myriad ways, with twinkle and texture, sparkle and shimmer.

FOR REFLECTION

What keeps you trusting in God?

Microwave Society

I use the microwave to cook most of my meals these days, and I expect food to be ready in 5 to 10 minutes, no matter what the entree may be. This expectation is part of a cultural phenomenon called microwave society, the mindset of wanting (and nearly getting) everything "right now." We do not put up with waiting.

As a result, patience has almost disappeared. We are restless and anxious. But the Bible reminds us that patience is necessary and beneficial: "Be patient, therefore, brothers, until the coming of the Lord. See how the farmer waits for the precious fruit of the earth, being patient about it, until it receives the early and the late rains" (James 5:7).

Patience makes what we are waiting for more precious. Waiting allows for growth and maturity. The people of God patiently waited for the arrival of Jesus, the Messiah, thousands of years after the promise was made. We are called upon to wait patiently for Jesus' Second Coming. In the nearly two thousand years that have passed since Christ's ascension, the Church has grown and matured and developed a closer relationship with our Savior. The wait will one day end with a harvest of blessings that can never be taken away: everlasting life with Christ. Isn't that worth the wait?

FOR REFLECTION

What are you most impatient about?

Fans

A Facebook question asked, "Do you use a fan at night?" I use an oscillating fan on low; the wind and the quiet sound help me sleep. The fan is a reminder of the Holy Spirit in my life. The Holy Spirit who came with a loud rushing wind on Pentecost continues to blow over me throughout my life, giving me peace, inspiration, strength and rest. The Holy Spirit guides my steps and gives me the words to say to others about the good news of Jesus Christ. Fans cool us down, and the Holy Spirit calms us when our souls are troubled and cools us down when we are hot under the collar about frustrations in life.

Scripture says, "The Spirit helps us in our weakness. For we do not know what to pray for as we ought, but the Spirit himself intercedes for us with groanings too deep for words" (Romans 8:26). The quiet sound of the fan points to the groanings of the Spirit expressed to God on my behalf.

Sometimes the work of the Holy Spirit is ignored, forgotten or taken for granted, but he is the driving force of our Christian life. If a little fan reminds me to celebrate the Holy Spirit's active role in my spiritual growth, then I am grateful.

FOR REFLECTION

How often do you think about the work of the Holy Spirit?

Showers

Recently the shower in my bathroom was not working; only a little water dribbled out. After many attempts to unclog the showerhead holes, I ended up buying (and installing, believe it or not!) a whole new showerhead. A strong, steady flow of water now pours out.

How many other things are clogged up in my life that need to be unclogged? Sadness clogs up the flow of joy. Anger blocks the way of love. Past frustrations stop me from trying again. How do we get unclogged? The prophet Hosea writes: "Let us know; let us press on to know the LORD; his going out is sure as the dawn; he will come to us as the showers, as the spring rains that water the earth" (Hosea 6:3). We need to let our God unclog what prevents us from moving forward. He showers blessings upon us that break through the barriers to a happy, holy life. It means an entire system replacement of our former way of life through spiritual renewal by the Holy Spirit. Daily, Jesus forgives us, digging out the gunk of sin building up in our lives.

The end result is a constant stream of goodness from above that refreshes our new life in Christ. Be made clean in him today!

FOR REFLECTION

What things have clogged up your relationship with God?

Songs from Prison

About midnight Paul and Silas were praying and singing hymns to God, and the prisoners were listening to them ... **ACTS 16:25**

Paul and Silas sang songs while other prisoners listened. We may be imprisoned by guilt, shame, sickness, chronic pain, grief, depression or loneliness. While we may just want to sing the blues, songs of praise to God are appropriate in prison. People are listening and watching. They see how we act in distress and hear what we sing in the dark cells of life.

Perhaps remembering his time in prison, Paul wrote, "I have learned in whatever situation I am to be content. I know how to be brought low, and I know how to abound. In any and every circumstance, I have learned the secret of facing plenty and hunger, abundance and need. I can do all things through him who strengthens me." (Philippians 4:11-13). Sharing joy with others when we are imprisoned by one thing or another lets people know that we have Christ on our side. We have forgiveness, eternal life, a relationship with our God, hope, faith, grace, prayer and strength. The strength of Christ can break through prison walls and restore any weary soul. That is something to sing about!

FOR REFLECTION

Do you sing the blues or songs of praise more often?

Trapeze Artists

Renowned spiritual author Henri Nouwen discussed what we can learn from trapeze artists. There is the moment that trapeze artists must let go of their own swing, trusting that their partner will be there at just the right time to catch them. For a second or two, the trapeze artist is dangling in midair, unattached to anything. Seconds like that can happen in our own lives, when we are between jobs or schools or nearing marriage, the birth of a child or retirement. That is when trust in God fills in the gaps until our God "catches" us on the other side of the transition and we find ourselves in the grip of his love and care for us.

When we fail to trust in God, we crash into things. We must never try to fly solo through life. Without God and his guidance, we can make a mess of things in our lives. With God's strength and power, we have a better sense of our purpose and plans in him. We have confidence in what to say and do, according to his will. And we find comfort in the fact that we have a God who lifts us up to safety and security that will never fail. All we need to do is let him carry us

FOR REFLECTION

When have you experienced God catching you?

Stones

In the Gospels, there are many references to stones. Jesus tells the scribes and Pharisees who want to kill an adulterous woman, "Let him who is without sin among you be the first to throw a stone at her" (John 8:7). On Palm Sunday Jesus says that if the people stop praising him, "the very stones would cry out" (Luke 19:40). In Gethsemane, Jesus goes "about a stone's throw" from his disciples to pray to his Father (Luke 22:41). When Jesus arises on Easter morning, the large stone in front of his tomb is "rolled back" (Mark 16:4). These stones in Scripture are reminders for us:

- We should not throw stones of judgment at others. We can be loving and forgiving.

- Rocks and trees and all the earth give glory to God just as we do. We blend our praise with theirs.

- Prayer should be personal and sometimes separate from those around us to focus our attention on God alone.

- Only the risen Jesus has the power to cast aside every heavy barrier that blocks us from a new relationship with him.

FOR REFLECTION

How is Jesus your Rock?

The Inner Circle

Jesus' inner circle of friends, Peter, James and John, joined him at good times (the Transfiguration) and bad times (Gethsemane). Jesus still had close relationships with the other disciples and followers, yet the inner circle shows our need for loved ones to whom we can turn in special or difficult times.

It is said that we are the average of our five best friends. What characteristics of your inner circle have become part of your own personality? Maybe it is a listening ear, a heart for God's Word or a welcoming nature. Christ is at the heart of any Christian circle of friends. How is he evident in your core group? Perhaps it is through prayer texts, times together at church or prayers at mealtime.

As he hung on the cross, Jesus told John and his mother to care for one another. He built an inner circle there, and in that moment, the two of them became family. The friends in my core group started calling each other "frienily"—a melding of *friends* and *family*. That is what we are in Christ, after all, brothers and sisters. And frienily does what family does. They are there for one another, through thick and thin. Thank God today for the family your friends have become for you through him.

FOR REFLECTION

Who are the members of your inner circle?

CHRIST-FILLED MOMENTS

Minnesota Nice

Minnesota Nice refers to the kindness of those who live in the Land of 10,000 Lakes. Minnesota Nice people are friendly, humble and willing to help. Minnesota Nice is an attribute that is so ingrained in a community that it has been given a name. Would *nice* be the first word that comes to mind when people think about Christians? Many other attributes may come to mind before *nice* when it comes to people's perception of the quintessential Christian. St. Paul wrote, "Be kind to one another, tenderhearted, forgiving one another, as God in Christ forgave you" (Ephesians 4:32). As Christians, we are called to go beyond nice. We are to be *tenderhearted*, which is translated from the Greek meaning "well compassioned and sympathetic." We should be richly *forgiving*, not judgmental. Forgiveness from the heart, as Christ forgives us, cannot be faked.

Jesus told us, "Let your light shine before others, so that they may see your good works and give glory to your Father who is in heaven" (Matthew 5:16). Our words and actions should not just show how nice we are, but they should point others to God in Christ. In Christ, we live to be a reflection of the heart and mind of Christ to the world. So be Christian Compassionate as well as Minnesota Nice.

FOR REFLECTION

How can you be Christian Compassionate today?

Erratics

Glacial erratics are found in my home state of Iowa and other places as well. Erratics are rocks, differing from native rocks, that are dropped by receding glaciers. Scientists sometimes use erratics to determine the movement of ancient glaciers. Erratics can be large or small and can be carried by glaciers for hundreds of miles from their original source.

Sometimes God places us far from where we started or where we thought we would be, and that may make us stand out from our surroundings. We are made up of different "stuff," spiritually speaking. Our faith in Jesus may set us apart as unusual or even an eyesore to unbelievers. Our place in life may seem erratic, but God settles us exactly where he wants us to be. Our presence in a certain area at a particular time may provide just the right opportunity for us to plant the love of Jesus. Our ability to endure tough circumstances may provide future strength for ourselves or others.

Life can be hard as a rock, but the enduring hope we have as God's new creations in Christ, no matter where we are, brings us peace and comfort. No place on earth is far from God.

FOR REFLECTION

Where has God placed you to make a difference?

Ministry of Presence

The Church is often, and rightfully, portrayed as a body at work, laboring in love for the Lord in hands-on activities. But there is just as much value in what is called the ministry of presence, just being there with someone in need. Our simple, physical presence can be a great gift to someone. We are there to talk if needed, or to be silent. We are available if some helpful task needs to be done.

My uncle once said about my aunt, "She was just always there." A couple from my parents' church sat in the waiting room with us while my dad was going through a complex surgery. They sat with us silently for hours and listened and responded to our concerns.

How can you take part in the ministry of presence? Maybe you can ask someone, "How is it going?" and listen to the answer, or you can watch TV with your mom to share that experience with her. Perhaps you can sit with a friend who hasn't been out of the house for a while. There's no need to prepare. Just let it happen. Your presence points to the constant presence of our Immanuel, God with us, who said, "I am with you always, to the end of the age" (Matthew 28:20).

FOR REFLECTION

Who needs your presence today?

Community

The concept of community has changed. It is much more broadly defined. A community is no longer just a group of people dwelling in close physical proximity or people regularly meeting together in person. A community can be a gathering of strangers and friends talking on a Zoom call from various locations in the country. A community can be people in their homes watching the same on-screen event. Community now means people united through a shared experience.

The Church must adjust to this new definition of community and accept that not all members are as drawn to the community of worship in the church building. Many are more comfortable participating in online Christian communities. Ways of "going to church" are more varied than they once were and continue to be reshaped.

This does not mean we stop cultivating community. As a Church, we must offer programs, events and worship experiences that are conducive to community. No gathering of believers should be left out in the cold. Open the door to every group that seeks to enter the community of faith happening around you. That can only lead to growth.

FOR REFLECTION

What communities are you a part of?

The Heart of the Matter

In the fourth century B.C., Aristotle believed that the heart was the center of the soul and that it affected emotions. People in the Middle Ages believed that goodness and holiness could be physically revealed in the heart. An enlarged heart, for example, meant that the person was loving and virtuous.

In our modern medical age, we know that the heart is a muscle that pumps blood, not the source of our emotions. Yet Jesus said, "You shall love the Lord your God with all your heart and with all your soul and with all your mind" (Matthew 22:37) and "Blessed are the pure in heart, for they will see God" (Matthew 5:8). The heart is seen as a site of love and spiritual wellness. But John reminds us, "God is greater than our hearts and he knows everything" (1 John 3:20).

God knows the beating of our hearts, the condition of our bodies and our reaction to events. Out of his own heart, he sent his Son to us that we might be free from the sin that makes our hearts ache. He warms our hearts and fills us with faith so that we may not be swayed by emotions but remain grounded in his grace. The heart of the matter in all things is Jesus.

FOR REFLECTION

How is your heart for God?

First Day of School

In August and September, social media is filled with photos of children standing in front of their front doors on the first day of school. A popular prop, especially in the early grades, is a first day of school "board" where children write their names, interests, family members' names, favorite things and what they want to be when they grow up. The boards are a quick snapshot of the child's personality.

Though our first days of school are long gone, it is good for us to remember that God's mercies "are new every morning" (Lamentations 3:23). Each day with the Lord is like the first day of school: new and fresh and full of possibilities. And each day we have a "board" we can complete in our minds with our name, family members' names, favorites, and hopes and dreams. Our review of who we are can remind us that we are baptized children of God, that we are blessed with family and friends and the wonders of this creation. We can start each day keeping God's plan for us in mind and learning new lessons from our Teacher every step of the way.

FOR REFLECTION

What would you put on your school "board"?

Save or Toss?

I once kept manuscript copies so I would have documentation of editing changes. This collection eventually filled 11 cardboard boxes stacked in my office as a monument to my hoarding tendency. A coworker suggested moving the boxes into storage, since all the files are safely saved on my computer. So off to storage the hard copies went. My office looks cleaner now, and my mind is not cluttered by worry that someone might need something from those boxes.

We hang on to many things far too long. Most people do not remember the time you made fun of someone in grade school. God does not keep a record of that, so you shouldn't either. You confessed, and you are forgiven.

The paperwork boxes also showed me that I was holding too tightly to my own achievements and my desire to prove my worth to others. But as the song by Keith and Kristyn Getty says, "My worth is not in what I own, but in the costly wounds of love at the cross." Only my place as God's forgiven child through Christ's death and resurrection will allow me to stand firm in this world and the next. I keep what is connected to Christ and I let go of the things of this world. Then my soul is at peace.

FOR REFLECTION

What are you holding on to too tightly?

Third Things

Education philosopher Parker J. Palmer coined the term "the third thing." The third thing is something outside ourselves that allows us to deepen our connection with another—a poem, a play, a movie, a TV show, a concert, a story, music or a work of art. A third thing might be shared experiences like doing the dishes or fishing together. "Rightly used, a third thing functions a bit like the old Rorschach inkblot test, evoking from us whatever the soul wants us to attend to. Mediated by a good metaphor, the soul is more likely than usual to have something to say," Palmer writes (*A Hidden Wholeness*, 93).

Jesus used a coin, a tree, a child, a trip to the well, a catch of fish and a mustard seed as third things to elicit a response in others. Jesus' use of third things drew people into the meaning of the kingdom of God, his relationship with his followers and living the spiritual life.

Most children's sermons utilize some sort of prop or visual aid as a third thing so children will engage more fully in the Gospel message. We can use third things to connect with our fellow Christians. Attend an event with someone or do a project with a friend. Who knows what conversations the Spirit may begin?

FOR REFLECTION

What third things have you used to connect with people?

CHRIST-FILLED MOMENTS

Places

My old high school building has become a middle school. My former grade school closed several years ago, and the building is vacant. My college dorm room is now a laundry room. A building where I once worked is now a storage facility.

Times change, places changes, but God puts us in specific places at certain times. The experiences we have are not about buildings but about the people we meet and the things we learn. So I hold on to the experiences I am having now and grow in my relationships with the people I know.

Look back to the past and give thanks to God for the people you encountered and the lessons you learned over the years. Then look at your life now. What is most meaningful to you? What will you remember? Hold these things close. Spaces may shift and the people around you may be different than before, but "every good gift and every perfect gift is from above, coming down from the Father of lights, with whom there is no variation or shadow due to change" (James 1:17). Every momentary place and passing person in your life is a gift. Savor these gifts from God in every stage of life.

FOR REFLECTION

What memories do you hold close?

Delays

In recent times we have experienced delays and shortages of things we have never known before. These shortages and delays have been caused by problems with the supply chain: not enough workers, trucks or equipment.

There is a lot of work to be done in the kingdom of God, but the Spirit works through people to accomplish that work. Jesus said, "The harvest is plentiful, but the laborers are few" (Luke 10:2). The Word of the Lord reaches hungry souls through those who serve in small ways—traveling, teaching, talking and carrying the Good News to the next place. If people stopped speaking the message of salvation in Jesus, the supply chain would derail and the Word would be delayed.

Every part of the chain of the spreading of the Gospel matters. "How then will they call on him in whom they have not believed? And how are they to believe in him of whom they have never heard? And how are they to hear without someone preaching? And how are they to preach unless they are sent?" (Romans 10:14-15). As each of us works for the Lord, the precious news of Christ's death and resurrection goes out to the world. Don't delay or slow the flow of the Good News of God's love and care.

FOR REFLECTION

What can you do to continue the flow of the Gospel?

Mysteries

You are the Christ, the Son of the living God.

MATTHEW 16:16

We all like a good mystery now and then. There is great satisfaction when we figure out what happened using the clues that we have been given.

An age-old mystery has been "Who is God?" People search high and low for the answer and come up empty. But we have God's clues revealed in the Old Testament. We have evidence in the miracles and messages recorded in the New Testament. We have the cross and empty grave that bear witness to the truth. Jesus is God, and he came to earth to save us through his death and resurrection. It is an open-and-shut case. No one can tell us otherwise. The God we seek has been found in the person of our Savior.

There may be other mysteries of life that we won't solve until we see Jesus in heaven. But the mystery that matters, the identity of the divine, is determined for us. The serpent in the garden said to Eve, "Did God really say … ?" (Genesis 3:1, NIV®). But through the Word of God we know that no questions or investigations are needed. We know the truth in Jesus and the truth has set us free.

FOR REFLECTION

How does it feel to know the truth of God?

Shook

The word *shook* can mean being shocked and surprised, rattled to your very core. When the angel Gabriel appeared to her, Mary "was greatly troubled" and "tried to discern what sort of greeting this might be" (Luke 1:29). Sounds like she was shook. And rightly so. On Christmas night, when the glory of the Lord shone round about them, the shepherds were "sore afraid" (Luke 2:9, KJV). They were shook. When Jesus rose from the dead, and the angel rolled back the stone of Christ's tomb, the soldiers guarding the grave literally trembled (see Matthew 28:4). If that's not shook, then I don't know what is.

In life we are often shook, perhaps upon the death of a loved one, the birth of a child or in a moving spiritual moment at church or in nature. It can be a frightening experience, but God can uplift you. Mary was blessed to be the mother of Jesus. The shepherds shared the Good News of Jesus' birth. Those who saw Jesus' empty tomb were filled with great joy at his resurrection, knowing that death was defeated.

We should not be afraid when shook. God will make things happen in his way and his time for our benefit. He may shake things up so we will be uplifted in his love and care.

FOR REFLECTION

When were you last shook?

Math

I was never very good at math, although I did make it through high school algebra by the skin of my teeth. Jesus asks us all to do a little math when Peter asks him, "Lord, how often will my brother sin against me, and I forgive him? As many as seven times?" Jesus said to him, "I do not say to you seven times, but seventy times seven" (Matthew 18:21-22). If my math is right, Jesus is asking us to forgive a person 490 times.

But Jesus doesn't want us to forgive someone 490 times and then refuse to forgive once that magic number is reached. Jesus is expressing an infinite number. Seven was seen as a perfect number (that is why Peter suggests it), so multiplying a perfect number by a multiple of a perfect number meant that the number of times we should forgive should be perfection upon perfection, a never-ending amount.

We can be a very unforgiving people. "I will never forgive him!" someone may say. But in Christ we have been renewed in the image of God. Forgiveness is in our spiritual DNA, with no number that calculates the end of our forgiveness. The number of times we say "I forgive you" is always countless.

FOR REFLECTION

How free are you to forgive?

Plugged In

When I moved my computer from my home office to my work office, I plugged all the cables and cords back into their appropriate outlets and ports, or so I thought. I had no internet until I discovered that one cable was plugged into the wrong port. I made the switch, and I was off and running.

Often the smallest things can disconnect us from God as well. When we plug into caring more about ourselves, the things of this world and our own personal stories instead of plugging into the story of salvation found in Scripture, we disengage from God. Things may seem to run along well, but at some point our screens go blank and we cannot move forward with the work we are to accomplish in the kingdom of God. Prayer and Bible reading establish our connection once more. We receive the wonderful messages of his love and care, his promises to be with us and his covenant to save us through the life, death and resurrection of his Son, Jesus.

Staying connected to God means that our operating system is optimal on all levels. Remember that even when your connection is unplugged or weak, God has never disconnected from you.

FOR REFLECTION

What helps you most to stay plugged in to God?

Holy Ground

Do not come near; take your sandals off your feet, for the place on which you are standing is holy ground.   EXODUS 3:5

From the burning bush, God told Moses that he was on holy ground. Moses took off his sandals to listen to God's command—go to Pharaoh and tell him to let God's people go from Egypt. It was a sacred space, a monumental experience for Moses. Heaven touched earth, and God's presence and will were made known.

We, too, stand on holy ground at significant times in our lives—at the birth of child, at the deathbed of a loved one, at the altar when we become a husband or wife, when a perfect job opportunity is placed before us, when we move to a new location or when a Bible verse alters our approach to living. While we do not need to take off our shoes when these things happen, we do need to sense more deeply God's mighty presence on earth. Our purpose and plan take on a new form in these moments. Our dependence on God comes to the forefront. We cannot do the holy work before us on our own, so we put our trust in the Holy One who empowers us all. Stay grounded in the holiness of God.

FOR REFLECTION

What holy ground have you stood on recently?

Peacemakers

Blessed are the peacemakers, for they will be called children of God. MATTHEW 5:9 (NIV®)

In the Beatitudes, Jesus calls us to peacemaking. This means that we are commissioned to mend divisions, reunite the opposed and bind up the broken. With so many warring factions in our world today, it is almost impossible to know where to start. We learn from Jesus to start small and start with what is close to us. Jesus brought peace to his disciples when they were fighting over who was the greatest (see Mark 9:33-35). In squabbles among friends and family, we can be the voice of peace, reminding all to be humble, as Christ was humble.

Another way to mediate is to interject love and compassion into the situation, as Jesus did when he embraced the children the disciples tried to send away (see Mark 10:13-16). Simple expressions of care can calm people down and bring them together. Speaking of God's desire in Jesus for all people to dwell in peace can help people put their differences aside (see 2 Corinthians 5:18-19; Psalm 133:1).

Not every dispute can be resolved, of course, but James writes, "Peacemakers, when they work for peace, sow the seeds which will bear fruit in holiness" (James 3:18, JB). Sow seeds of peace today and see what happens.

FOR REFLECTION

What seeds of peace can you sow today?

CHRIST-FILLED MOMENTS

Generations

One generation shall commend your works to another, and shall declare your mighty acts. PSALM 145:4

There are seven living generations in the United States:

- Greatest generation (born from 1901 to 1926)

- Silent generation/traditionalists (born from 1927 to 1945)

- Baby boomers (born from 1946 to 1964)

- Generation X (born from 1965 to 1980)

- Millennials/Generation Y (born from 1981 to 1996)

- Generation Z/iGeneration (born from 1997 to 2012)

- Alpha generation (born from 2013 to 2025)

I am a member of Generation X. My grandparents, of the Greatest generation, taught me by example through church attendance and daily devotions. My parents, of the Silent generation, enrolled me in a Christian school and prayed with me. My Baby boomer school teachers taught me to memorize Bible verses and learn Christian songs. Each generation has a new way to share Jesus. How can you share the Gospel?

FOR REFLECTION

What actions do you identify with the most?

Homeless Jesus

On the campus at Valparaiso University in Indiana is a bronze sculpture called *Homeless Jesus*, by artist Timothy Schmalz. It depicts Jesus, identifiable by the wounds on his feet, wrapped in a blanket and sleeping on a street bench. The image portrays the words of Jesus in Matthew 25:35-45, in which he explains that when we care for the sick, poor, naked, hungry, thirsty, imprisoned and strangers, we are really caring for him.

The statue is convicting. Often I have looked the other way, walked on the other side of the street or turned around completely when I have come near a homeless person. The statue reminds me that Jesus is present where we do not want to go. We are called to say a word of blessing, give a granola bar or bottled water, or provide a gift card to someone in need.

It is important to stay safe, but it is also important to extend our comfort zones. Jesus did not steer clear of "the least of these." He touched lepers. He spoke to beggars. He ate with sinners. No one was beyond his care. We must not shrink back in fear but reach out in faith. God will use us to bring relief to a hurting world, one precious person at a time.

FOR REFLECTION

What can you do to help the homeless?

Speech Acts

Speech acts present information and perform an action, such as promising, ordering, warning or inviting. A couple saying, "I do," witnesses swearing an oath in court or our confession of sins are all speech acts that change the reality of a situation. God used speech acts at creation:

> "Let there be light," and there was light.   GENESIS 1:3

> "Let the earth bring forth living creatures according to their kinds—livestock and creeping things and beasts of the earth according to their kinds." And it was so.   GENESIS 1:24

When God speaks, things happen. Jesus, God the Son, proclaims: "Be healed," and people are healed, "You are forgiven," and sins are removed, "I am with you always," and he is.

Jesus, the Word made flesh, succeeded in the thing for which God sent him (see Isaiah 55:11). The Word is at work in baptism: "I baptize you in the name of the Father, and of the Son, and of the Holy Spirit." The Lord speaks in Holy Communion: "Take and eat; take and drink." Reality changes through these speech acts: children of earth become children of God; partakers of blessed bread and wine are united with Christ. The Word of the Lord speaks into existence our relationship with him. "Let the word of Christ dwell in you richly" (Colossians 3:16).

FOR REFLECTION

What can you say to bring about change for the better?

Faces

We live in an era in which we think more often about each other's faces. Many faces appear before us when we video chat with family and coworkers. There are faces we can't see behind masks in grocery stores or restaurants. Our faces are on our profile pictures on Facebook, Instagram and other social media outlets.

Face it! Our faces say a lot about us, about who we are, how we feel and what matters to us. It is important for our faces to reflect Christ. The Bible says, "For God, who said, 'Let light shine out of darkness,' has shone in our hearts to give the light of the knowledge of the glory of God in the face of Jesus Christ" (2 Corinthians 4:6). Our faces should shine with Jesus' love. Our faces should show that we know the way out of the darkness. No matter what we face, we have a Savior who watches over us with love and leads us to glorify him in every smile, every listening ear and every eye that looks with care. People say they can see people smile through their masks. The beauty of our faith in Christ can shine through any barrier. Let your face be a beacon of Christ's presence in your life.

FOR REFLECTION

What helps you face challenges in your life?

Repurposing

On home improvement shows, old crates are repurposed as rustic coffee tables; old school lockers become bookshelves. Artists create art pieces from kitchen utensils, tins and toys from flea markets and antique stores.

The conversion of St. Paul is a story of repurposing. He was zealous in his persecution of Christians until God repurposed that zeal to proclaim the Gospel. Like a craftsperson, God can create something beautiful and unexpected from our random skills.

We may be struggling with purpose: Am I in a dead-end job? Do I have skills that are unused or underused? Am I feeling unfulfilled in my tasks? Go to God in prayer: "Repurpose me! Use me in a new way as a follower of Christ." God will open your eyes to new opportunities. "Behold, I am doing a new thing; now it springs forth, do you not perceive it? I will make a way in the wilderness and rivers in the desert" (Isaiah 43:19). God can redirect your efforts in more energizing and meaningful ways.

If you were once a teacher, you might teach a Bible class. A former roofer might volunteer to repair the church roof. Each of us can be repurposed by God. Let God show you where and why. "For everything there is a season, and a time for every matter under heaven" (Ecclesiastes 3:1).

FOR REFLECTION

What is God repurposing you for?

Extra

In modern use, the word *extra* can mean "excessive, dramatic behavior; doing the absolute most." If someone decorates a birthday party with so many balloons you cannot see the floor, we could say that person is being extra.

Scripture tells us how extra our God is. He is "able to do far more abundantly than all we ask or think" (Ephesians 3:20). Jesus talks about the gifts we receive as "a good measure, pressed down, shaken together and running over" (Luke 6:38).

God's love is extra. As the contemporary song "One Thing Remains" by Jesus Culture professes, "Your love never fails. It never gives up. It never runs out on me." We don't deserve God's love, yet he gives us more than enough. As God's forgiven and free people, we are reminded, "from his fullness we have all received, grace upon grace" (John 1:16, NIV®).

Be a little extra in response to God's goodness. Can you give a little extra in your offering? Can you give a little extra time helping your children with their homework? Can you be a little extra caring to your spouse? A little can go a long way. Just ask the boy who had a little extra food to share, food that Jesus used to feed a multitude.

FOR REFLECTION

What makes God extra to you?

Restart

We have all been there. The computer stops working and we are at a loss as to what to do to remedy the situation. We ask computer experts what elaborate protocol might be necessary to fix the problem, only to be asked, "Have you tried restarting?" The simple act of turning your computer off and on again is sometimes all that is necessary to resolve the glitch.

When we are broken down or just not working as we should in life, the psalmist tells us to restart:

> *Bless the LORD, O my soul,*
> *and forget not all his benefits,*
> *who forgives all your iniquity,*
> *who heals all your diseases,*
> *who redeems your life from the pit,*
> *who crowns you with steadfast love and mercy,*
> *who satisfies you with good*
> *so that your youth is renewed like the eagle's.*
>
> **PSALM 103:2-5**

Make it a practice to restart your remembrance of God every time you must restart your computer. The benefits are abundant.

FOR REFLECTION

What gifts of God do you need to recall most often?

Left Turns

Left turns are some of the most difficult driving maneuvers, especially on a busy road with traffic moving at a fast pace in both directions. Making a left turn is risky, requiring skill, boldness and quick thinking. That is why, for a time and at the bemusement of my friends and family, I avoided making left turns at all costs, even if it took me longer to get somewhere. I just didn't want to take the risk. I have since returned to making left turns, becoming more patient with a driving task I once avoided.

Jesus never avoided taking "left turns." He took risks and did not turn away when lepers cried out for healing, when a blind man pleaded for mercy, when Pharisees came to him with questions. He did not take the easy way and turn away from the cross. He faced the distress and pain that lay ahead.

Jesus wants us to be risk-takers, too. He wants us to turn to those who need our help and talk to people who have questions about our faith. He wants us to take up our cross and follow him. Avoiding left turns is not an option in the Christian life. In fact, taking left turns, taking risks and chances, is what Christianity is all about. Turn left today!

FOR REFLECTION

What risk can you take for the Gospel today?

CHRIST-FILLED MOMENTS

Imprinting

In a phenomenon known as imprinting, a young animal narrows its social preferences to an object (typically a parent) to which it is exposed. It is most obvious in chickens and geese, who imprint on their parents and then follow them around. Scientists discovered, though, that geese often imprinted on the first moving stimulus of any kind within the critical period of 13 to 16 hours after hatching. Goslings waddled behind a human being or followed a box-covered model train circling a track.

Through the work of the Holy Spirit in baptism, we imprint on our Savior and follow him wherever he goes. Our path in life mirrors his as we go about preaching, teaching, praying, loving and caring as he did. Scripture says, "Therefore be imitators of God, as beloved children. And walk in love, as Christ loved us and gave himself up for us, a fragrant offering and sacrifice to God" (Ephesians 5:1-2).

Sometimes we lose our way and imprint on family, friends or coworkers, or on inanimate objects—cars, homes, work, computers, television, hobbies and pastimes. Such imprinting can lead us in false directions.

Imprint on your Savior by reading his Word and using your hands and feet to echo his. The more we are exposed to him, the more we imprint on him. Follow Jesus.

FOR REFLECTION

What impression has Christ made on your life?

Bible-Bingeing?

In recent years, the time people spent watching shows and movies on streaming services rose sharply, especially binge-watching—viewing a series of movies or episodes of a show one after the other at a single sitting or over several days in a row.

How might we apply the same principle to Bible reading? Could we engage in Bible-bingeing, if you will, as part of our daily routines? There are many reading plans for studying Scripture, but I am thinking about our general approach to Bible reading. Do we set aside chunks of time for study? Are we excited to dive deeply into Scripture?

We can find a million and one reasons not to read our Bibles these days. But now we need the Bible more than ever. Its true stories of God's people express betrayal, reunion, suffering, triumph, learning, growing, and ultimately salvation in our Savior Jesus, the happy ending to our lives. Sounds like some of the shows we binge-watch, doesn't it? But biblical stories guide us more than any TV show can.

Why not try some Bible-bingeing? Choose a book or a section of Scripture to read in blocks of time over a period of days. Let the Holy Spirit move you to read the Bible with new-found curiosity and joy. Let the Bible-bingeing begin!

FOR REFLECTION

What can motivate you to read the Bible more?

The Aaron

Many people seek fame, but often it is better for us to be the Aaron. We may be called to be like Aaron in the Bible, who served in a supporting role to his brother, Moses. During a battle, God told Moses to stand on a hill with his arms raised to bring victory to Israel. As the battle raged on, Moses grew tired. Aaron stepped in to hold up Moses' arms until the Israelites were victorious.

For whom can you be the Aaron? Who needs support and strength as they battle illnesses or injuries, difficult situations or enemies of God? You can hold their hand or lift their spirits when they are ready to give up. You can remind them that the victory is ours in Jesus Christ, who saves and forgives us.

Do you know those who need encouragement to carry out what God has in mind for them? You can speak words of assurance to them, speak on their behalf or work together with them. As St. Paul wrote, "Encourage one another and build one another up, just as you are doing" (1 Thessalonians 5:11).

Sometimes it takes just one person to make things happen. Be the Aaron for someone. Work behind the scenes to let God's work be revealed. Let Christ's servant love be known through you.

FOR REFLECTION

Whom can you lift up today?

Leaves

He told them this parable: "Look at the fig tree and all the trees. When they sprout leaves, you can see for yourselves and know that summer is near. Even so, when you see these things happening, you know that the kingdom of God is near." LUKE 21:29-31

On my bike rides, I noticed more leaves on the ground than usual. I realized it was the end of August and fall was near. The thought occurred to me that no matter what is going on in our lives, the seasons still change.

The leaves on the ground reminded to be more attentive to the signs of things to come that God puts in my path, even when I am encountering earthly upheavals in my life. He puts Bible verses in front of me: "Surely there is a future, and your hope will not be cut off" (Proverbs 23:18). God warms my face with the sun to remind me that the Son of God warms my heart.

Keep your eyes open for the messages Christ sends you as trees turn colors and leaves fall. There is glory yet to be revealed and our lives will change forever on the Last Day when Jesus returns. There is no stopping his arrival, just as there is no stopping the changing of the seasons. Keep watch.

FOR REFLECTION

How has nature drawn you closer to Christ?

CHRIST-FILLED MOMENTS

Deepening Gratitude

The concept of gratitude shifts as we grow older. As children, we are grateful for the things we have—family, our friends, home, school, toys, clothes, meals and snacks. But as the years go by, we look beneath the surface. We are more grateful for the healing at work within ourselves and one another. We become more grateful for the trust we have in God and the strength he grants us.

You may not know what is going on in the lives of others, but God does, and his grace is at work. People may not know everything going on in your life, but God's grace is at work inside of you too. This is also a reason to be grateful.

Our hearts are opened more than ever to the outpouring of God's love. Thanksgiving is not just about a big meal. It is about being close to our Savior and filled with confidence and comfort. Our joy overflows into an expression of thanksgiving that is from the heart. God's gifts are far richer than we could ever have imagined as a child. Let that richness flow into our conversations, prayers and actions and reflect in our smiling faces as we gather in our homes at tables of God's goodness.

FOR REFLECTION

What are you most grateful for today?

Prepare

The Church sets aside the weeks of Advent to prepare for the birth of Christ on Christmas. There are many things you can do to get ready for Jesus. You can count down the days on a calendar, light candles on an Advent wreath, read daily seasonal devotions and attend special worship services in your church.

The most important thing is to prepare your heart for Jesus. You can discard those things that distract you from the Christ Child. You can make Jesus a priority in your personal decisions and planning. With Jesus at the center of your life, you will follow his will and his way. As John the Baptist said, "He must increase, but I must decrease" (John 3:30). What Jesus wants must take precedence over what you want. His life must become the driving force of your life. In Advent you can hand the reins of your life to Jesus and let him steer the course of your future.

Advent is deeper than candles, candy and decorations. It is about total dependency on Christ. It is about becoming a vessel in which he lives. It is about letting him be mangered in you.

FOR REFLECTION

How does it feel to be a dwelling place for Christ?

Steals on the Ear

In my favorite hymn, "For All the Saints," a certain phrase caught my attention:

> And when the strife is fierce, the warfare long,
> **Steals on the ear** the distant triumph song,
> And hearts are brave again, and arms are strong.
> Alleluia! Alleluia!

Steals on the ear? What does that really mean? The word *steal* in this context means to move quietly or surreptitiously. That "distant triumph song" is moving quietly and secretly onto our ears. While we are surrounded by all sorts of noisy sounds in our lives, a far-off tune beckons us to the victory celebration in heaven, where the saints surround the throne of Christ and praise him for saving us from sin, death and hell forever. The word reminds us of the experience of Elijah, who heard God not in the wind, the earthquake or the fire, but in the still, small voice that Elijah strained to hear.

What sounds steal on your ear amid all the hustle and bustle of Christmas? We hear jingle bells and Christmas carols and holiday commercials, but to what should our ears be attuned? Listen for the distant cry of a baby in a small town thousands of miles—and centuries—distant. The whisper of God will steal on the ear: "I love you!" Listen for it!

FOR REFLECTION

When have you heard the still, small voice of God?

Cloth Christmas Tree

The message that Christ has come for "all the people" makes me think of a tabletop cloth Christmas tree I bought at a little gift shop in St. Charles, Missouri. It is made of felt squares of different colors and sizes stacked on top of one another to create a festive Christmas tree shape.

Each of us is like a square of cloth, brought together with other squares of cloth to celebrate the good news of great joy for all the people. It does not matter if you are young or old. It does not matter what race or region of the world you are from. It does not matter whether you are on the top or at the bottom of society. We all join as one to create something beautiful to welcome our Savior. We all point to the star, who is Jesus, the Light of our lives and the pinnacle of our existence.

At Christmas, take a look around at the people celebrating with you and singing a beautiful carol together in praise of the Christ Child. Say the lovely words of a prayer in unison to glorify the One who has come to deliver us all from sin, death and the devil. Join as one to uplift the Son.

FOR REFLECTION

What can you do to join with others in Christ?

Ornaments

I enjoy buying Christmas ornaments from places that I visit. One year, on my vacation to Wisconsin, I found a metal ornament in the shape of the state with a cutout of a hiker in the middle. It perfectly encapsulated my experience of hiking in various parts of the state and rejoicing in God's creation. I have enjoyed putting that ornament on my Christmas tree each year since.

What experience do you want to remember fondly from the past year as you celebrate Christmas? The fact is, Christ comes to us in various ways, not just at Christmas but throughout the year. What "Christmas ornament" moment do you want to rejoice in today? What moment do you want to give thanks to God for?

Christmas is a day to remember that Jesus Christ was born to save us from sin and death forever. His love decorates our lives year after year. The beauty of his birth is precious to us and something that we need to celebrate. Let this Christmas be the beginning of many more Christmas moments throughout the coming year, moments when we see the love of our Savior ornamenting our world.

FOR REFLECTION

What reminds you of a special time you shared with Jesus?

Protection

On December 24, 2017, on my way to Iowa for Christmas, the car in front of me started spinning out, causing me to start spinning out in the snow. I ended up facing the opposite direction of traffic on Interstate 270 in St. Louis, but I did not hit a single car and I was able to turn the car around and pull off, unhurt, to the side of the road. After pulling myself together, my only thought was that God was protecting me.

There are moments in our lives when we wonder if God is watching over us, but in that moment I knew for certain that he was. There is really no other explanation for how I (and my car) escaped that situation unscathed. The words of Psalm 20:1 were fulfilled in my life that day: "May the LORD answer you when you are in distress; may the name of the God of Jacob protect you" (NIV®).

Now I find myself much more grateful for safe travel and much more aware of the small blessings God grants to us every day out of his sheer mercy and love for us. He is always looking out for us. I found that out firsthand. Thank God today for all the ways that he protects you!

FOR REFLECTION

When have you felt protected by God?

CHRIST-FILLED MOMENTS

Manger Scene

During the season of Advent my family would always have a little manger scene set out. It was a child-friendly set, with a stable that looked like Lincoln Logs and Fisher-Price-style figures (I know I am dating myself with these references). This manger scene was a wedding gift for my parents, who were married over 50 years ago on December 27, 1967. What a wonderful wedding gift to give: the story of the birth of Jesus in tangible form to share with future children. My parents still have those figures, and they still put them out. When I see them, I am reminded of the marvelous story of Christ, who came to earth to save us. We need to share that story with family and friends every Christmas, year after year. It is a story we need to treasure with all our hearts.

To this day, one of the wise men in the set never stands up right. He always is tipping over. He is perpetually in a state of bowing to the Christ Child. That is what we should do. In everything we say and do at Christmas, we can continually worship Jesus. That is our place in the manger scene!

FOR REFLECTION

How can you share the story of Jesus with others?

Christmas Moments

There are always special Christmas moments: children running down the stairs to find presents under the tree, families gathered around the dining table for a delicious dinner, phone calls (and maybe Zoom calls) from distant relatives. I hope and pray your Christmas includes one or more of these moments.

But the most important moment for me on Christmas Day has been my father's reading of the Christmas story in Luke 2 from the King James Bible. That moment centers me in what the day is all about: Jesus and the story of his humble birth amid animals and angels, shepherds and straw, to save us all. The story is not flashy, but it frames everything we do. Just as God gave us the gift of his Son, we give gifts to one another. Just as shepherds ran to be with Jesus, we travel to be with one another. Just as angels sang in the sky, we speak messages of peace and goodwill in person or through satellite connections in space.

Jesus came at just the right moment, that all our moments might be special because of him.

FOR REFLECTION

What Christmas moments are special to you?

Stay Here

When the year ends, many people consider what new adventures they would like to enjoy in the new year or they plan major changes in their lives. While this may be beneficial in some circumstances, sometimes the best plan is to stay where you are.

Before Jesus ascended to heaven, he said to his disciples: "I am sending upon you what my Father promised; so stay here in the city until you have been clothed with power from on high" (Luke 24:49, NRSV). Jesus wanted the disciples to stay where they were until the Holy Spirit came and moved them to venture out into new locales. The disciples listened: "They stayed continually at the temple, praising God" (Luke 24:53, NIV®).

Sometimes the best thing to do in life is to stay here. Be at peace where God has placed you. Do not pine for some other location that sounds more appealing. The Holy Spirit will tell you when it is time to move. In the meantime, spend time in worship, prayer and service to others. Who knows what God has in store for you right where you are?

FOR REFLECTION

What helps you stay content with where you are?

Christ-Filled Moments
PRAYERS

For Comfort
Soothe my troubled and wearied soul, O Lord, with your comfort. Surround me with your presence. Ease my mind with your promises of hope and assurance. Take away the worry and fear that entrap me, and fill me to overflowing with peace and confidence in you to carry me through. Amen.

For Guidance
Direct me in the way that you would have me go, O Savior. Beckon me toward the path that is meant especially for me. Help me to listen to your call and see your hand at work in leading me to understand what is best for my life of faith. I trust in you alone to travel with me in my journey ahead, so divinely designed to bring me closer to you. Amen.

For Faith
Give me faith in you, dear Jesus Christ, faith that is solid and firm, faith that is confident and lasting. Let nothing shake my faith, but in everything, may my faith in you grow stronger and deeper. By the Holy Spirit, may I be inspired to show and share my faith freely and joyfully, in good times and in bad, in hardship and in triumph. For without faith, I know I have nothing at all. Amen.

For Awareness

Dear Jesus, keep my eyes open to your work in the world, and keep me aware of the impact your presence has on me and my surroundings. Grant me a sense of what you desire for me in certain situations and circumstances, and fill me with the knowledge that you are an integral part of every aspect of my life. May all I am seek to know you more. Amen.

For Grace

Ever-giving Jesus, pour your grace and goodness upon me as I strive to live as your disciple. Forgive my sins which have led me away from you. Lift the burdens of guilt and shame that have slowed me down in my service for you. Shower me with your undeserved love so that I might be a blessing to those around me and a true follower of your will. May I consider everything a marvelous gift from you. Amen.

For Growth

O Savior, continue to help me grow in my faith in you. Help me to expand in my knowledge of you more day by day. Open my mind to new opportunities to serve and live as your disciple. By following your example, I come to know more fully what living for you means. Keep my heart open to being stretched in my commitment to you and provide me with paths to divine discoveries about my place and purpose in this world. Amen.

Christt-Filled Moments
TOPICAL REFERENCES

Booklets with Gospel Bites

Whether you are looking for ways to fit God's encouraging Word into an overwhelming schedule or wondering how to connect seekers to accessible content in a meaningful way, these booklets use well-known Scripture verses to draw readers to the Heavenly Father who cares for all our needs and shares all our concerns.

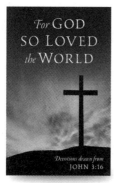

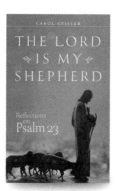

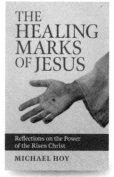

FOR GOD SO LOVED THE WORLD
(GL3)

THE LORD IS MY SHEPHERD
(LD6)

HEALING MARKS OF JESUS
(HLJ)

QUANTITY	1	2-99	100-499	500-1499	1500+
PRICE	$1.49	$0.99	$0.85	$0.65	$0.49

BOOKLET PRICING IS NOW ASSORTABLE FOR MIX-AND-MATCH PRICING.

Learn more at **CreativeCommunications.com**